CITYSPOTS
MARS

WHAT'S IN YOUR GUIDEBOOK?

Independent authors Impartial up-to-date information from our travel experts who meticulously source local knowledge.

Experience Thomas Cook's 165 years in the travel industry and guidebook publishing enriches every word with expertise you can trust.

Travel know-how Contributions by thousands of staff around the globe, each one living and breathing travel.

Editors Travel-publishing professionals, pulling everything together to craft a perfect blend of words, pictures, maps and design.

You, the traveller We deliver a practical, no-nonsense approach to information, geared to how you really use it.

ABOUT THE AUTHOR

Born in the United States, Kathryn Tomasetti grew up in Italy and studied in Great Britain. She currently calls the historic port of Nice in the South of France home, just two hours away from Marseilles (or five hours away on her red scooter). Kathryn is an avid traveller, and has penned articles and authored guidebooks covering the whole of Mediterranean Europe. Her background in the art world and her passion for food makes cours Julien Kathryn's first stop on any visit to Marseilles.

CITYSPOTS
MARSEILLES
Kathryn Tomasetti

Thomas Cook

Written by Kathryn Tomasetti

Published by Thomas Cook Publishing
A division of Thomas Cook Tour Operations Limited
Company registration No: 1450464 England
The Thomas Cook Business Park, 9 Coningsby Road
Peterborough PE3 8SB, United Kingdom
Email: books@thomascook.com, Tel: +44 (0)1733 416477
www.thomascookpublishing.com

Produced by The Content Works Ltd
Aston Court, Kingsmead Business Park, Frederick Place
High Wycombe, Bucks HP11 1LA
www.thecontentworks.com

Series design based on an original concept by Studio 183 Limited

ISBN: 978-1-84157-907-8

First edition © 2008 Thomas Cook Publishing
Text © Thomas Cook Publishing
Maps © Thomas Cook Publishing/PCGraphics (UK) Limited
Transport map © Communicarta Limited

Series Editor: Kelly Anne Pipes
Production/DTP: Steven Collins

Printed and bound in Spain by GraphyCems

Cover photography (Marseilles' Harbour) © Mark English/Alamy

CONTENTS

SYMBOLS KEY

The following symbols are used throughout this book:

ⓐ address ⓣ telephone ⓕ fax ⓦ website address ⓔ email
ⓛ opening times ⓝ public transport connections ⓘ important

The following symbols are used on the maps:

ⓘ information office   ▢ points of interest
✈ airport   O city
✚ hospital   o large town
🛡 police station   ○ small town
▣ bus station   = motorway
▤ railway station   — main road
Ⓜ metro   — minor road
✝ cathedral   — railway
❶ numbers denote featured cafés & restaurants

Hotels and restaurants are graded by approximate price as follows:
£ budget price ££ mid-range price £££ expensive

Abbreviations used in addresses:
av.   avenue
blvd   boulevard
pl.   place (square)

◑ *Jules Cantini's monumental marble fountain graces place Castellane*

Introduction

Marseilles is a vibrant, bustling city. All the usual South of France attractions are apparent – the blue skies, the beaches with their turquoise waters and the picturesque fishing villages – but Marseilles seems to offer its visitors so much more, and by that we don't just mean *bouillabaisse* and *pastis*. The capital of Provence-Alps-Côte d'Azur region, Marseilles is the second-largest city in France, and enjoys a competitive rivalry with Paris. Its 810,000 residents are spread over 111 villages within the city limits, divided into 16 *arrondissements* (boroughs). Marseilles is the largest port in France, the eighth-largest in the world, and much like other buzzing seaside cities, it has an edgy, transient, all-things-are possible feel. It's often been called the 'Gateway to the Orient', an indication of the exotic promise it suggests as much as a reference to its geographical location. The city's demographics are hugely varied, with over a third of the city ethnically Italian, a quarter French, a quarter North African and the third-largest Jewish community in Europe. Combine this variety with the boisterous students attending the University of Provence and the large number of people who come to live in the city because they've heard of its various pleasures, and the result is an active and expanding counter culture. Renowned artists like Cézanne, Braque and Renoir all painted in Marseilles at the turn of the century, but unlike the somewhat stagnant art scene on much of the French Riviera, Marseilles is currently experiencing a constant growth in the arts. The city's pop music and hip-hop scene is one of the foremost in France. Bold and defiant, Marseilles is the city that created the French national anthem *La Marseillaise* during the country's Revolution. Marseilles is also the perfect location to use as a base to discover surrounding inland and coastal towns.

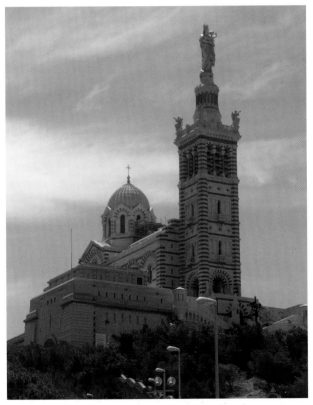

● *Notre-Dame de la Garde protects fishermen and locals alike*

When to go

Visit Marseilles between May and July, when the mistral has tapered off and the weather is sunny yet fresh, perfect for exploring the coast and the nearby Calanques (see page 104). Summer sees the city's residents flood into the streets for festival after festival – check the Annual events (see page 12) to plan a visit during those that pique your interest. As is common in the South of France, some of Marseilles' renowned local businesses shut up shop in August, so if you're hankering after a particular meal, item or night out, be sure to check seasonal closures in advance.

SEASONS & CLIMATE

Like other towns on the Mediterranean, Marseilles' winter days (Jan–Feb), are humid and average around 12°C (54°F). Summer days (July–Aug) are hot and dry, with an average temperature of 29°C (85°F). The city is affected enormously by the mistral, or cold winds that funnel down from the Alps, so be sure to pack a light, wind-proof jacket, no matter what the season. The sun is often even hotter than it seems, so make sure you are slathered with sunscreen during the summer months, as the wind often makes the temperature seem cooler, and it's easy to get burned without realising it.

● *Explore rugged coastlines and dip into the crystal waters of the Calanques*

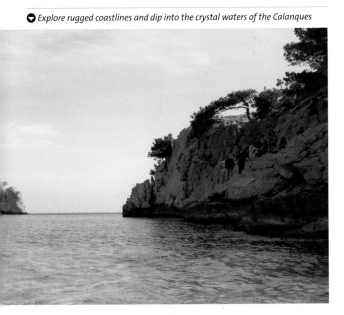

ANNUAL EVENTS

Marseilles has a lot to celebrate, and events take place throughout the year, with the highest concentration of festivals occurring during the warmer months. The city's most popular events focus on music and the arts.

February
Chandeleur (Candlemas) This candlelit procession at dawn, featuring a walnut statue of the Virgin Mary, Notre Dame de Confession, ends at the Saint-Victor Abbey on 2 February.
Ⓦ www.marseilles-tourisme.com
Open 13 This tennis tournament, on the APT Tour, is one of the most popular events for European players.
Ⓦ www.open13.org

February & March
Carnaval (Marseilles Carnival) Each of Marseilles' neighbourhoods is represented by a float in the city's themed Carnival parade, which starts on La Canebière or avenue Prado and finishes at the Parc Borély. Ⓣ 04 91 55 37 95 Ⓦ www.marseilles-tourisme.com

March & April
French Winegrowers' and Farmers' Spring Fair Celebrate spring as producers from all over France gather to show off their wines, organic produce and cured meats at the Parc Chanot.
Ⓣ 04 42 56 66 83
Russian Festival Organised by the Théâtre Toursky, performances and exhibitions are dedicated to Russian culture and the arts (see page 33).

April

SNIM (International nautical week) Check out the international regatta off Marseilles' shores, organised by the Société Nautique de Marseilles. ⓦ www.lanautique.com

April & May

Festival de la musique sacrée (Festival of sacred music)
Free concerts and performances take place frequently over a month-long period. ⓐ Saint-Michael Church, 1 pl. de l'Archange ⓦ www.marseilles-tourisme.com

June

Ciné Plein-Air (Open-air cinema) There are outdoor showings of classic and contemporary films on cours Belsunce, cours Julien and the Panier district right through until the end of August. ⓦ www.cinetilt.org

Marseilles Pride The massive gay pride parade departs from the Parc du 26e Millénaire, and continues with an evening party of dancing and top DJs. ⓦ www.citegay.fr

July

Bastille Day (14 July) Check out the fireworks (ⓐ Vieux Port ⓛ 22.00) as well as rocking celebrations of France's national day throughout the city.

Festival International de Folklore This festival celebrates traditional customs and dance from all over the world. ⓐ Château Gombert ⓦ www.marseilles-tourisme.com

Festival de Marseilles The month-long festival celebrates Marseilles and its place in all disciplines of the cultural arts, and is centred around the Vieux Port. ⓦ www.festivaldemarseilles.com

Festival de Jazz des 5 continents (Five Continent Jazz Festival)
This electrifying worldwide celebration of jazz attracts some
of the best players on the planet. ⓐ Parc Longchamp
ⓦ www.festival-jazz-cinq-continents.com

Mondial à Pétanque (World Pétanque Tournament) Top
international players compete for the title of World Pétanque
(French boules to some) champion. ⓦ www.petanque.org

Les Nuits Caroline (Caroline Nights) Hop on a boat to the
Frioul Islands for live music, cinema and dancing in the open-air
auditorium (formerly the Caroline Hospital). ⓐ Frioul Islands

August
Joutes de l'Estaque (Estaque Jousting Competition) Teams battle
it out to poke and prod each other into the sea at the Port de
l'Estaque. ⓐ Port de l'Estaque ⓦ www.marseilles-tourisme.com

September
La Foire (The Fair) This massive international fair has been going
for over 80 years, and features arts, food, crafts and games.
ⓐ Parc Chanot ⓦ www.foiredemarseilles.com

Marsatac Possibly the largest electronic and techno music
festival on the Mediterranean, this gathering attracts many
international DJs. ⓐ quai J4 ⓦ www.marsatac.com

October
Fiesta des Suds A festival of Mediterranean music, dancing, food
and more. ⓐ Docks des Suds, Joliette ⓦ www.dock-des-suds.org

Marseilles-Cassis Semi-marathon For the enthusiastic (and fit) runner, this semi-marathon covers some staggering heights. ⓦ www.marseille-cassis.com

December
La Foire aux Santons (Nativity figurine fair) Get ready to start decking out your Nativity Scene, with inspiration from the hand-painted clay figurines at this fair. ⓐ cours d'Estienne d'Orves ⓦ www.foire-aux-santons-de-marseille.com

---

PUBLIC HOLIDAYS
Le Premier de l'An (New Year's Day) 1 January
Pâques (Easter) & Lundi de Pâques (Easter Monday) 23–4 March 2008, 12–13 April 2009
Fête du premier mai (Labour day) 1 May
Fête de la Victoire (WWII Victory day) 8 May
L'Ascencion (Ascension) 1 May 2008, 21 May 2009
La Pentecôte (Pentecost/Whit Sunday) & Lundi de Pentecôte (Whit Monday) 11 & 12 May 2008, 31 May & 1 June 2009
Fête nationale (Bastille day) 14 July
Assomption (Assumption of the Blessed Virgin Mary) 15 August
La Toussaint (All Saints Day) 1 November
Jour d'armistice (Remembrance Day) 11 November
Noël (Christmas Day) 25 December

Euroméditerranée project

Never a wallflower when it comes to urban architecture, Marseilles is upping its game to an even higher level with a programme of drastic, fantastic urban regeneration that's known as the Euroméditerranée project.

This project has attracted many big-name participants. The Joliette Docks (see page 66) have been renovated by the architect Eric Castaldi, and now house the offices of 300 blue-chip companies. The French container transport company CMA-CGM is building an amazing 29-storey skyscraper designed by the unconventional 'deconstructivist' Zaha Hadid. Those who prefer more traditional architecture should reach for their smelling salts when her vision is realised: already one can see how the 110-m (361-ft) structure is toying with curved lines and asymmetrical angles. The nearby Les Terrasses du Port will transform port buildings into shops and leisure facilities, and surrounding squares will be decked out in urban foliage. The Euromed Centre will house a Marriott hotel complex, an urban park and a multiplex cinema. Director Luc Besson is leading this project.

Architect Yves Lion is concentrating on the new Cité de la Méditerranée, which will span the seafront from Fort Saint Jean to the new public gardens to the north, in the Arenc. The J4 pier will be renovated into the Pôle St Jean (or St Jean Centre), with an expansive esplanade and open public spaces. It will house the new Centre de la Mer (Sea Centre), and the Museum of European and Mediterranean Civilisations, which will be redesigned by Rudy Ricciotti. Like its name, the design for the museum borrows elements from a range of European cultures, facilitating their

⬥ *The Euroméditerranée renovation of the Joliette Docks (artist's impression)*

interplay with dramatic results. An IMAX cinema, an aquarium, restaurants and bars will also be opened in the Cité de la Méditerranée.

There's no point being daring if there's no-one around to be shocked, so the Gare Saint-Charles and Porte d'Aix areas will also be redeveloped. With new high-speed TGV train links to the city, Marseilles is striding towards its goal of making visitors' eyes pop and jaws drop the very second they see the city. The Euroméditerranée project is due to be completed by 2016, by which time the Joliette will most certainly be ready for its close-up.

For more information ⓦ www.euromediterranee.fr

History

Ligurian tribes were the first known residents of what is now Marseilles and the surrounding coastal areas. In 600 BC, Greek explorers from Phocaea (Asia Minor) arrived in the area. According to legend, Naan, the local Ligurian tribal chief, prepared a feast to welcome the explorers. By a quirk of fate, this feast occurred on the exact day that his gorgeous daughter, Gyptis, was to choose a husband from a pack of local suitors. Unable to resist the swarthy charms of Protis, one of the explorers, Gyptis offered him a flask of water to indicate her choice. Protis married into the family, and the happy couple received the land around the port as a wedding gift. They founded the port of Massalia, which went on to become one of the period's most important trading posts.

By the days of the Roman Empire, the city had been renamed Massilia and was the centre of Mediterranean commerce,

🔽 *Explore the Parc and Palais du Pharo, Napoleon III's former residence*

prospering as the main port of trade between the Romans and central Europe. In the 12th century, ships from Marseilles ferried crusaders to the Holy Land, and it was during this time that the city adopted what is still its flag, a blue cross on a white background.

Things took a downward turn for Marseilles in the 14th century, when it was the portal through which Black Plague entered Europe, decimating the population. In 1660, King Louis XIV redeveloped the city's fortifications, allowing the urban centre to spread further south and inland. The town was a centre of resistance during the French Revolution, rallying the country with the national anthem, La Marseillaise. During the mid-19th century, the city's commercial port moved just around the corner to La Joliette, and in 1905, an ironwork transporter bridge was installed across the Vieux Port. Destroyed in 1947, there is now a small ferry that takes foot passengers across the port. Ever a city at the forefront of drama, King Alexander I of Yugoslavia was assassinated in Marseilles in 1934, and was one of the first assassinations ever to be filmed. During World War II, much of the city was bombed by Nazi forces, including a huge portion of the Panier district (see page 60). The city centre was rebuilt after the war with contributions from the German and Italian governments. Marseilles has always had a high influx of immigrants, particularly in 1962 from Algeria post-independence. In the 1970s, the city was affected heavily by gangs, mafia and soaring crime levels, although this has changed significantly in recent years. With the ongoing Euroméditerranée project, many of the poorer areas of the city are being revitalised, and Marseilles is slowly becoming one of the most vivacious cities in the South of France.

Lifestyle

Although it could give a lot of other cities master-classes in
relaxation, Marseilles is still a busy, buzzing, living-and-working
city. Head to the markets in the morning and you'll see locals
bustling off to work, stopping to gulp down a quick coffee or
maybe to grab a newspaper. However, the general pace of life
differs greatly when compared to Northern Europe, or even
Paris. A little more time is taken, a few extra minutes are given
over to a friendly exchange (pleasant behavioural traits that
may be due to the warmer temperatures or the soothing effect
of the nearby Mediterranean). In any case, the city's tempo provides
a valuable lesson in slowing down and savouring life.

Whether you are visiting for work or for a long weekend, it's
best to take care of errands in the morning, when business and
markets are up and at 'em, and leave the afternoons (especially
in summer) for wandering explorations or simply chilling out
and watching the world go by. Family time is important, as is
taking time to eat, talk and relax with loved ones. The best way
to understand the city is to watch what's going on around you.
Don't be afraid to chat, and if you're lucky, you may receive
friendly advice or some crucial insider information.

Because of its location on the sea, and the fluctuations
in immigration from all over the world, Marseilles' religious
population is far from homogeneous. Most ethnically French are
Catholic, but the city is also home to close to 200,000 Muslims
and has a large Jewish community.

Marseilles' cost of living is lower than that of nearby Aix-en-
Provence, or coastal towns in the vicinity. You can expect to pay

around €1.50 to sit down with a coffee, as compared to €2.50–3.00 in other cities nearby. Hotels also reflect this price difference, with places located in the city often costing less than those in the more touristy towns in the area.

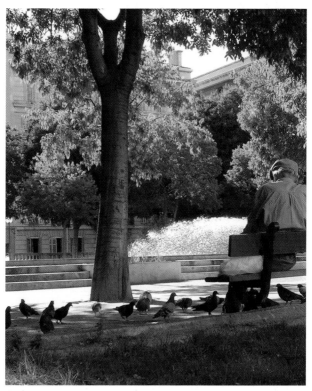

⬤ *Follow the locals' lead and relax in one of the city's many parks*

Culture

From being named one of France's Villes d'Art (governmental recognition of the city's dedication to the arts) to the new museums, cinemas and even the aquarium planned as part of the Euroméditerranée project (see page 16), Marseilles' cultural activities span the gamut from classic to contemporary.

The city is home to 20 museums, including the exceptional modern art collection at the Musée Cantini (see page 83), and myriad public monuments. Notre-Dame de la Garde, Saint-Victory Abbey and Cathédrale de la Major draw religious devotees by the thousands. Marseilles' Opera House was the second to be built in all of France. Do visit Port de l'Estaque, a fishing harbour on the north side of the city, where Cézanne, Braque, Renoir and others painted at the turn of the century, squeezing in a couple of *chichi freggi* (fried doughnuts that are an Estaque speciality) while you're there (Ⓜ Metro: 2 to Joliette, then bus: 35).

Marseilles boasts one of the most avant-garde scenes in France. Theatre productions at La Criée (see page 75) win awards every year and La Friche de la Belle de Mai (see page 89) is fabulous for sampling some of the city's unique offerings. Check out **FRAC**, or Fond Régional d'Art Contemporain (ⓐ 1 pl. Francis Chirat ⓣ 04 91 91 27 55 ⓦ www.fracpaca.org), which organises contemporary art exhibitions at their centre in the Panier district. The city is also home to some of the best French hip-hop, with local groups like IAM topping charts throughout Europe.

Get updated as to what's going on by picking up one of the free local magazines, like *Trottinette* or *What Magazine Urbain*, which are often stacked outside shops or in the tourist office.

◔ *Visit Le Corbusier's futuristic housing complex, the Cité Radieuse*

You can take advantage of all that Marseilles has to offer with the outstanding-value *City Pass*. Costing just €20 for one day or €27 for a two-day pass, this booklet of coupons offers free entry to all the major museums in Marseilles, as well as the Château d'If (see page 64). A transport pass is also included, covering all public transport for the duration of the *City Pass*, as well as free trips on each of the city's two **Petit-Train routes** (ⓐ quai du Port ❶ 04 91 25 24 69 ⓦ www.petit-train-marseille.com Ⓜ Metro: 1 to Vieux-Port). Alternately, for an overview of the city's major cultural sights hop on **Le Grand Tour** (ⓐ quai du Port ❶ 04 91 91 05 82 Ⓜ Metro: 1 to Vieux-Port; €20 two-day pass, €17 one-day pass, €8 child under 11).

▶ *Access quai de Rive Neuve via the passenger ferry outside the town hall*

Shopping

The city's main shopping district spans from rue Paradis on the west side, to rue de Rome on the east, and is bordered by La Canebière on the north and place Castellane on the south. Hit these main streets and squares for well-known French and international brands like Naf Naf, Princess Tam-Tam, H&M, Kookai and Galeries Lafayette. The **Centre Bourse** shopping centre (🄰 17 pl. Belsunce 🅆 www.centre-bourse.com 🄻 09.30–19.30 Mon–Sat 🄼 Metro: 1 to Vieux-Port; bus: 21, 31, 32, 41S, 57, 61, 70, 80, 89, 97; tram: 1 to Belsunce) also includes branches of many mainstream stores, like Habitat, Marionnaud and Body Shop. Veer onto the smaller cross streets off rue Paradis, like rue Vacon and rue Grignan, for upscale boutiques like Cartier or Galerie Cargo. Rue de la Tour has been nicknamed 'Rue de la Mode' (or 'Fashion Street'), and is now home to a wealth of local designers, including Manon, Diable Noir and Empreinte du Sud. To pick up a pair of Marseilles' own 'Le Temps des Cerises' jeans, head to their flagship boutique in rue Haxo. Created in 1998, this local brand has rocketed in popularity worldwide.

Don't miss the tiny shops that line cours Julien and the narrow streets in Le Plaine – they often stock offbeat wares, including an excellent selection of used books and CDs, that you won't find elsewhere in the city. The Quartier des Antiquaires, a short walk from place Castellane, often throws up an unusual gift.

Markets are everywhere, and a few of the best are the daily Fish Market on the Vieux Port, the Brocante Market on avenue du Cap Pinède (see page 70 for details to both), the Organic

USEFUL SHOPPING PHRASES

What time do the shops open/close?
A quelle heure ouvrent/ferment les magasins?
Ah kehlur oovr/fehrm leh mahgazhang?

How much is this?
C'est combien?
Cey combyahng?

Can I try this on?
Puis-je essayer ceci?
Pweezh ehssayeh cerssee?

My size is ...
Ma taille (clothes)/ma pointure (shoes) est ...
Mah tie/mah pooahngtewr ay

I'll take this one, thank you
Je prends celui-ci/celle-ci merci
Zher prahng serlweesi/sehlsee mehrsee

Market on cours Julien and the Marché des Capucins
(see page 84 for both).

Marseilles' local specialities include Marseillaise soap, olive
oil, wine, nativity figures, *pastis* and *navettes* (biscuits flavoured
with orange blossom, see page 99). All of these items can be
purchased at speciality stores throughout the city.

Eating & drinking

Eating and drinking are serious and passionate activities in Marseilles.

The aperitif culture is strong here. One is taken before dinner, usually between 18.00 and 20.00, and is said to 'open' the stomach, in preparation for the meal that follows. The favoured aperitif is the city's own *pastis*, an anise-flavoured alcoholic drink diluted with water that was invented either by drinks magnate Paul Ricard or by a monk. In any case, when absinthe was declared illegal in 1915, the local population was looking for a new drink to replace their favourite beverage. *Pastis* more than sufficed.

The next tier of Marseilles' culinary culture is *bouillabaisse*. Originally a fish stew made by fishermen in order to use up their market leftovers, this traditional Marseillaise recipe has become a gourmet's staple. Normally a maximum of six types of fish are stewed in a tomato and saffron broth. Diners eat the soup first, with croutons and *rouille* (a garlic pimento mayonnaise), before delving into a mountain of fish, which has been sliced and dished up at the table. There are just 11 restaurants internationally (one each in Paris and Switzerland, the rest in Marseilles) that adhere to the Charte de la Bouillabaisse

PRICE CATEGORIES
Prices are per person, for an average three-course meal, excluding wine.
£ up to €30   ££ €30–50   £££ over €51

Marseillaise, an agreement as to what constitutes 'true' *bouillabaisse* – for the real deal, check that the restaurant has posted the 'Charte' indication outside.

If the thought of travelling home to a land without *bouillabaisse* fills you with dread, why not book a professional *bouillabaisse* lesson? You may not be able to purchase quite the same ingredients, but the lessons will teach you how to make this intense fish soup like a true Marseillaise. Alternately, foodies

◔ *Enyoy a* pastis *on the tiny balcony at La Caravelle*

A FISHY TALE

According to the Charte de la Bouillabaisse Marseillaise, the word *bouillabaisse* comes from the cooking instructions, 'quand çà bouille... abaisse (le feu)', meaning 'when it boils, lower the flame'.

can also choose to assist a gourmet chef in his restaurant for the day, shadowing the action and picking up tips and recipes. (Both can be reserved through the tourist office, €110 per person.)

Unsurprisingly, Marseilles is also home to a vast array of ethnically diverse restaurants, reflecting the population of the city itself. In particular, be sure to try the tagines and couscous served throughout the city at authentic Moroccan and Tunisian restaurants – the recipes are some of the finest you'll taste outside of North Africa.

Most restaurants are normally open for lunch from 12.00 to 14.30 and for dinner from 19.30 to 22.30, although they may serve throughout the day, or later into evening in the centre of the city. Tipping is not essential, as service is almost always included (unless stated on the menu e.g. *service non compris*). However, if you've enjoyed your meal, it's polite to leave a few euros; 10% is considered generous. At a bar, it's common courtesy to leave €0.20–0.50, or your extra change.

If you are on a tight budget, you can still sample Marseilles' delectable treats. Head to one of the city's Produce Markets (see page 100), and pick up a selection of fresh fruits and vegetables, cheeses, salami and hams. Grab a baguette or two, and if the weather's fine, take your picnic to the Parc du Pharo. Sip a glass of local wine, kick back and enjoy some of the finest views in the city.

USEFUL DINING PHRASES

I would like a table for ... people
Je voudrais une table pour ... personnes
Zher voodray ewn tabl poor ... pehrson

Waiter/waitress!	**May I have the bill, please?**
Monsieur/Mademoiselle!	L'addition, s'il vous plaît!
M'sewr/madmwahzel!	*Laddyssyawng, sylvooplay!*

Could I have it well-cooked/medium/rare please?
Je le voudrais bien cuit/à point/saignant?
Zher ler voodray beeang kwee/ah pwang/saynyang?

I am a vegetarian. Does this contain meat?
Je suis végétarien (végétarienne). Est-ce que ce plat contient de la viande?
Zher swee vehzhehtarianhg (vehzhehtarien). Essker ser plah kontyang der lah veeahngd?

Where is the toilet (restroom) please?
Où sont les toilettes, s'il vous plaît?
Oo sawng leh twahlaitt, sylvooplay?

Entertainment & nightlife

Marseilles has a well-deserved reputation for offering some of the very best entertainment and nightlife in the South of France. While other nearby holiday destinations, such as Cannes and Saint-Tropez, tend to target primarily those with money to burn and sunglasses to wear at night, Marseilles offers visitors a heady mix of year-round concerts, theatre, bars and clubs, most of which is easily affordable, even to those on a budget. On the right kind of balmy night, Marseilles is fun city numéro un.

For films in English, try **Varietes**, just off of La Canebière
(37 rue Vincent-Scotto ☎ 08 92 89 28 92 Ⓜ Metro: 2 to Noailles;
tram: 1 to Canebière-Garibaldi). Theatres like **La Criée** (see page 75),
the **Gymnase** (a 4 rue Théâtre Français ☎ 08 20 00 04 22
ⓦ spectacle.lestheatres.net Ⓜ Metro: 2 to Noailles; tram: 1 to
Canebière-Garibaldi) and the **Toursky** (a 16 promenade Léo Ferré
☎ 0 820 300 033 ⓦ www.toursky.org Ⓜ Metro: 2 to Bougainville;
bus: 72, 89, 97) all offer exciting nights of drama, dance and
music. If ballet is what really grabs you by the tutu, check

⬥ *Head to the vibrant cours Julien for late-night bites*

● Marseilles is a bustling Mediterranean city at any hour

ⓦ www.ballet-de-marseilles.com for the local troupe's seasonal performances (ⓐ various locations), while opera performances can be seen at the city's Opera House (see page 84).

The terraces surrounding the Vieux Port and the place aux Huiles are ideal spots to quaff an aperitif and have a chat as the sun goes down. Most of the year, La Friche de la Belle de Mai (see page 89) organises an eclectic mix of concerts and club nights. Le Plaine, and specifically the cours Julien area, tends to dominate the alternative late-night scene (which is highly alternative and frequently very late), with bars sometimes spilling out into the pedestrianised squares. In the summer, you could do a lot worse than follow the locals' lead and head down to the Prado beach area, where outdoor activities, street performers and musicians abound. Prado is a tremendously groovesome location these days. Marseilles is also renowned for its local hip-hop scene, and big names, such as IAM, have worked their way up through the urban ranks and gone on to achieve international fame. Live music of all genres is often available at bars and locales throughout the city, and there are many unforgettable gigs performed by people you've never heard of (and never will again – here, entertaining is not exclusively about forging a career).

Marseilles receives a constant boost of energy from its large and youthful student population, and much of the nightlife is geared toward this demographic, with bars closing around 01.00 and clubs often pumping wicked tunes until the wee, small hours – packing up the hot stylus at four in the morning or even dawn is far from unheard of. However, there are plenty of options for the more grown-up crowd, including cocktail bars like the Caravalle (see page 73), live jazz (see Pêle-Mêle, page 74) and loads of fine dining.

Pick up one of the free weekly newspapers, such as *What Magazine Urbain*, or check Ⓦ http://marseillebynight.com for the best picks of what's currently happening in the city.

Sport & relaxation

With its prime location on the sea and a balmy climate year round, it's no wonder that Marseilles has more than its fair share of sports and outdoor activities.

SPECTATOR SPORTS

Love to watch but not so keen to participate? Catch one of local team Olympique de Marseilles' football matches at the **Stade Velodrome** (ⓐ 3 blvd Michelet ⓣ 04 91 76 56 09 ⓦ www.om.net ⓜ Metro: 2 to Rond-Point du Prado; bus: 21, 22, 23, 41S, 44, 45, 72, 83). Hardcore fans can also visit the team's museum (see page 98) or arrange a guided tour of the stadium (contact the tourist office for details). Marseilles' rugby team, Marseilles Provence XV, also plays at the Stade Velodrome. Alternatively, head to the coast to catch one of the regattas, like the SNIM in April (ⓦ www.lanautique.com) or Septembre en Mer (ⓦ www.officedelamer.com), or check out Les Voiles du Vieux Port in June (ⓦ www.lesvoilesduvieuxport.com).

PARTICIPATION SPORTS

To learn to sail or enquire about fishing, contact the **Club Nautique** (ⓐ SNM Pavillon Flottant, quai de Rive-Neuve ⓣ 04 91 54 32 03 ⓦ www.lanautique.com ⓜ Metro: 1 to Vieux-Port), where you can also pick up information about the 15 sailing schools along the coast. If you'd rather learn to kayak or use one to explore Marseilles' inlets, try **Kayak Attitude** (ⓦ www.kayak-marseille.fr) or **Raskas Kayak** (ⓦ www.raskas-kayak.com). There are 36 diving schools in Marseilles – try Abyss (ⓦ http://abyssservices.com), or check ⓦ www.marseilles-tourisme.com for a full list and information as to how to organise a dive to the Red Coral Cave on the south side of the Maire Island. Rock-climbing is hugely popular in the nearby Calanques. If you have experience, ⓦ www.topo-calanques.com contains information on the lay of the land and paths to follow.

RELAXATION

If your idea of sport tends to be a somewhat less adventurous, the city offers plenty of options that are geared more toward relaxation rather than an adrenaline rush. Rent bikes at **Tandem** (ⓐ 16 av. du Parc Borély ⓣ 04 91 22 64 80 Ⓝ Bus: 19, 83). Head to **Borély Golf** (ⓐ 136 av. Clôt Bey ⓣ 04 96 14 01 40 Ⓝ Bus: 44) to practice your swing. Try one of Marseilles' spas or hammams, such as **La Bastide des Bains** (see page 71) or **Hammam Rafik** (ⓐ 1a rue de l'Academie ⓣ 04 91 54 21 62 Ⓝ Metro: 1 to Estrangin; bus: 21, 41S). Or if the sun is shining and the weather is fine, grab a novel and head to one of the city's beaches (see page 91).

🔺 *Swim, sail or simply sunbathe along Marseilles' coast*

Accommodation

Marseilles has a fairly wide range of hotels, although it may be difficult to find budget accommodation in the summer months or in the heart of the city centre. Try to book at least a few weeks in advance if you plan to travel to Marseilles in July or August – remember that these are the months when the French take their holidays, so the most charming places to stay may fill up quickly. Be sure to check the hotel's location carefully, as some of the cheaper options are often tucked away on poorly lit back streets near the train station; this area is undergoing a general 'smartening up', but it can still be somewhat sketchy at night. The most extravagant hotels are around the Vieux Port or along the corniche John Fitzgerald Kennedy.

Lutetia £ This pretty little hotel is the city's best budget option, although a little bit of a walk from the centre's bustling action. Free Wi-Fi access. ⓐ 38 allée Léon Gambetta ⓣ 04 91 50 81 78 ⓕ 04 91 50 23 52 ⓦ www.hotelMarseilles.com ⓜ Metro: 1 to Réformes; tram: 1 to Réformes

Alizé £–££ Directly on the Vieux Port, this hotel offers simple rooms in an 18th-century building. It's worth paying extra to

---

PRICE CATEGORIES

Prices are for double rooms, per night, not including breakfast.
£ up to €75   **££** €75–125   **£££** over €125

book a sea-facing room – the sunsets are divine. **a** 35 quai des Belges **t** 04 91 33 66 97 **f** 04 91 54 80 06 **w** www.alize-hotel.com **n** Metro: 1 to Vieux-Port

Le Péron £–££ Rooms individually decorated during the 1960s make this family-run hotel one of the most unusual in the city – kitsch yet stylish. Book a corner room, where you can see the sea from bed. **a** 119 corniche John Fitzgerald Kennedy **t** 04 91 31 01 41 **f** 04 91 59 42 01 **w** www.hotel-peron.com **n** Bus: 83

Saint-Louis £–££ Just off La Canebière, rooms have a Provençal country theme, with pale colours and white wood, and mattresses are of the highest quality. **a** 2 rue des Récolettes **t** 04 91 54 02 74 **f** 04 91 33 78 59 **w** www.hotel-st-louis.com **n**: Metro: 1, 2 to Noailles; tram: 1 to Canebière-Garibaldi

Unité d'Habitation, Hotel Le Corbusier £–££ A monument to post-World War II design, the Unité is both futuristic and simple. Somewhat unusual and quite a distance from the city centre, this is the spot for true architecture enthusiasts. **a** 280 blvd Michelet (shuttle bus from Gare Saint-Charles) **t** 04 91 16 78 00 **f** 04 91 16 78 28 **w** www.hotellecorbusier.com **n** Metro: 2 to Rond-Point du Prado; bus: 21, 22, 23, 41S, 44, 45, 72, 83

Bellevue ££ Most famous for the aperitifs served at its first-floor Caravalle bar (see page 73), the Bellevue offers simple rooms on the edge of the Panier district. To date there is no website and reservations cannot be made by internet. **a** 34 quai du Port **t** 04 96 17 05 40 **f** 04 96 17 05 41 **n** Metro: 1 to Vieux-Port

Hotel du Palais ££ The Hotel du Palais has plain, cheerful rooms, and is centrally located, within walking distance of the Old Port and city's main shopping areas. Staff are exceptionally helpful. ⓐ 26 rue Breteuil ⓣ 04 91 37 78 86 ⓕ 04 91 37 91 19 ⓦ www.hotelmarseilles.com ⓝ Metro: 1 to Estrangin; bus: 41S

Le Rhul ££ One of the founding fathers of the official Charte de la Bouillabaisse Marseillaise (see page 28 or check the website, below), Le Rhul is perched on the sea, with views to die for. Sit back and watch the boats drift by. ⓐ 269 corniche John Fitzgerald Kennedy ⓣ 04 91 52 01 77 ⓕ 04 91 52 49 82 ⓦ www.bouillabaissemarseille.com ⓝ Bus: 83

Mercure Beauvau Vieux Port £££ Very well located, this hotel is the oldest in the city, undergoing an entire renovation in 2004. George Sand and Chopin chose to stay here when they eloped in 1839. Very good views over the Vieux Port from the hotel's bar. ⓐ 4 rue Beauvau ⓣ 04 91 54 91 00 ⓕ 04 91 54 15 76 ⓦ www.mercure.com ⓝ Metro: 1 to Vieux-Port

Le Petit Nice £££ For a weekend of total extravagance, head to Le Petit Nice. Owned by the Passedat family since 1917, the hotel has 15 sea-facing rooms spread over 2 neo-Greek villas. Dine in the gorgeous garden, swim in the heated seawater pool or make use of the free bikes to explore the city. A favourite of the very rich and famous. ⓐ anse de Maldormé, corniche John Fitzgerald Kennedy ⓣ 04 91 59 25 92 ⓕ 04 91 59 28 08 ⓦ www.petitnice-passedat.com ⓝ Bus: 83

🔺 *Spoil yourself at the sumptuous Le Petit Nice*

Tonic Hotel £££ This plush joint finished its massive renovations in 2007, and now offers streamlined, modern rooms with internet access and flat-screen TVs, directly on the Vieux Port. ❸ 43 quai des Belges ☎ 04 91 55 67 46 🖷 04 91 55 67 56 🕸 www.hotels-de-marseille.com Ⓜ Metro: 1 to Vieux-Port

THE BEST OF MARSEILLES

Whether you're breezing through town on the way to another Provençal destination or dedicating days toward exploring the city, Marseilles offers activities and sights to suit all its visitors.

TOP 10 ATTRACTIONS

- **Château d'If** Take a boat trip to visit the castle that was immortalised in *The Count of Monte Cristo* (see page 64)

- **La Friche de la Belle de Mai Complex** This is a fascinating place to catch a gig or simply meander through its winding alleys (see page 89)

- **Joliette Docks** Check out some serious (if wacky) urban regeneration here (see page 66)

- **Notre-Dame de la Garde** This wonderful cathedral (also known as 'La Bonne Mère') is not only beautiful itself: so are the views across the city that it offers (see page 95)

- **Panier district** Stroll through the evocative lanes of the original medieval quarter of the city (see page 60)

- *Pastis* **sipping** Just the one on the Vieux Port's quayside terraces while watching the yachts drift in simply has to be done (see page 28)

- **Parc du Pharo** Grab that picnic hamper and head up to this beautiful spot which offers amazing views of the Vieux Port (see page 95)

- **Quai des Belges** Get up early and see this fish market, one of the few remaining spots in the south of France where fishermen sell their own morning catch (see page 70)

- **Savonnerie** A visit to one of these intriguing factories shows how Marseilles soap is produced (see page 85)

- **Savour bouillabaisse** Taste this local dish exactly as it's meant to be at one of the nine spots in Marseilles which adhere to the strict 'Charte de la Bouillabaisse Marseillaise' (see page 28)

🔽 *Stroll the winding streets of Panier, the city's stunning medieval quarter*

Suggested itineraries

HALF-DAY: MARSEILLES IN A HURRY

Head down to the Vieux Port to check out the local fisherman hawking their morning catch on the quai des Belges (see page 70),

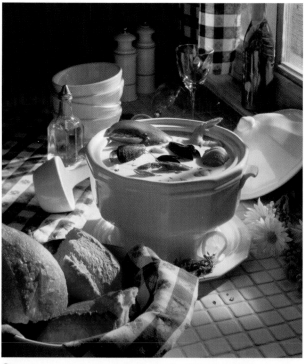

🔴 *Any itinerary allows time to savour an authentic* bouillabaisse

then take in modern art at the Musée Cantini or urban fashion at the Musée de la Mode, both within easy walking distance (see page 83). Finish with the city's most famous dish, *bouillabaisse*, at the Miramar (see page 74).

1 DAY: TIME TO SEE A LITTLE MORE

If you have the rest of the day free, work off that massive lunch with a hike (or take the Petit-Train) up to the Notre-Dame de la Garde (see page 95) for incredible views over the city. In the evening, head to La Caravelle (see page 73) in the Hotel Bellevue, and enjoy a *pastis* on their tiny balcony. Hit the cours Julien area for dinner and a taste of local nightlife.

2–3 DAYS: TIME TO SEE MUCH MORE

If the weather is fine, take one of the frequent ferries to the Château d'If (see page 64), or spend a lazy afternoon on Les Catalans beach or the Prado seafront (see page 91). The following day, head in the other direction, wandering through the Panier district (see page 60) for an eventual exploration of the Joliette Docks (see page 66).

LONGER: ENJOYING MARSEILLES TO THE FULL

With a chunk of time at your disposal, be sure to visit the Port l'Estaque fishing harbour, where Cézanne, Braque and other artists painted (see page 22). Alternatively, head to the Vieux Port and take a boat tour of the Calanques, or hop on the train for a day trip to Cassis (see page 104) or Aix-en-Provence (see page 116).

Something for nothing

With a little bit of planning, it's easy to have a great time in
Marseilles while spending very little money. Walk to the public
beaches, like Les Catalans, and spend the afternoon swimming
and people-watching. Or stroll along the corniche John Fitzgerald
Kennedy to the seaside monuments, like the Monument aux Morts
des Armées d'Orient (see page 95) and contemporary French
artist César's Monument des Rapatriés d'Algérie (see page 95).
Explore the colourful cottages in the picturesque Vallon des Auffes
(see page 96), also within walking distance of the city centre.
The Parc du Prado (see page 94) attracts street performers,
and there are beautiful parks all over the city, from the Pharo,
to Longchamp, to Borély (see pages 95, 80 & 134), each one filled
with walking paths and activities for children and adults. For the
price of a bus ticket (€1.70), catch one of the buses departing from
place Castellane for the Calanques, and spend the day hiking in
a tropical paradise.

Window shop your way down La Canebière and rue Paradis,
checking out the wares in the Quartier des Antiquaires (west of
rue de Rome and spreading south behind the Prefecture), or explore
the centuries-old squares of the Panier district. Browse through
the city's many markets, noting the seasonal produce or searching
for the perfect bargain. Visit Savonnerie de la Licorne for a free
tour of a traditional Marseillaise soap factory (see page 85).
Municipal museums are free the first Sunday of every month,
while other museums, such as the contemporary exhibitions at
FRAC (see page 28) or the Musée Boutique de l'OM (see page 98)
in the Stade Velodrome, are free all of the time. Wander around

⬤ *The picturesque port and cottages of Vallon des Auffes*

the courtyard of the Vieille Charité (see page 68), or gaze at the Jardins des Vestiges (see page 82), visible for free from the walkway between Centre Bourse and rue Barbusse. In summer you can catch free outdoor cinema at various locations. Or why not just linger for hours at a café table in the Vieux Port, watching the world go by?

When it rains

When the rain is pouring down (or the mistral is blowing so hard you can no longer stand it), Marseilles offers a huge array of indoor activities that will make you quickly forget the weather outside. Choose your area of interest and head to one of the city's many museums. Musée Cantini (see page 83) often shows free documentary films to accompany their exhibitions, so if your French is fairly fluent, sit down and enjoy the show. Alternatively, head to Varietes (see page 33), just off of La Canebière, for films in English. For die-hard shoppers, the rain may present the perfect excuse to spend hours in the Centre Bourse shopping centre (see page 26), including the onsite branch of Galeries Lafayette. It's still possible to enjoy a tour of the city's sights from the inside of Le Grand Tour (see page 24), the sightseeing bus that departs from the Vieux Port, hopping off to explore the cavernous insides of the Notre-Dame de la Garde Cathedral (see page 95), then catching the next bus passing by. Go underground to visit the crypts in Saint Victor Abbey (see page 96), or check out what's going on at the huge La Friche de la Belle de Mai (see page 89), which is largely self-contained. If the chill is getting to your bones, visit one of the city's hammams, like La Bastide des Bains (see page 71) for a scrub and a steam, followed by a cup of fruit tea.

On a rainy evening, why not choose a cosy restaurant, and enjoy a relaxed meal and fine wine in good company? Honoré (see page 100) has a warm atmosphere, delicious tapas and an eclectic mix of items for sale in their boutique at the back; or choose one of the portside restaurants for scalding bowl of *bouillabaisse*. The city's theatres and the Opera House (see page 84) offer a wide range of different performances throughout most of the year (except during the peak of summer), each one sheltered from the elements.

🔺 *Mosaics shimmer inside the Notre-Dame de la Garde Cathedral*

On arrival

TIME DIFFERENCE

Marseilles follows Central European Time (CET). At the end of March the clocks are put ahead one hour, then put back at the end of October.

ARRIVING

By air

Marseilles Provence Airport is to the northwest of the city, in Marignane. It has two terminals: major carriers use Terminal 1, while Terminal 2 serves low-cost carriers. ⓐ Marignane ⓣ 04 42 14 14 14 ⓦ www.marseille.aeroport.fr, www.mp2.aeroport.fr

Taxis are located outside the arrivals hall of Terminal 1. The journey to the city centre costs about €35–40.

Airport Taxis ⓣ 04 42 88 11 44 or 04 42 14 24 44 ⓦ www.taxis-aeroport.com

By rail

The main train station, Gare Saint-Charles, provides direct routes to all major French cities. Local trains serve Aix-en-Provence, as well as the coast and the entire south of France.

SNCF Gare Saint-Charles ⓐ rue Honnorat, pl. Victor Hugo ⓣ 3635 (in France), 08 92 35 35 35 ⓦ www.sncf.fr ⓜ Metro: 1, 2 to St-Charles

By road

Buses are the most economical way to arrive in downtown Marseilles and they leave every 20 minutes (ⓛ 05.30–21.50) for

IF YOU GET LOST, TRY ...

Excuse me, do you speak English?
Excusez-moi, vous parlez anglais?
Ekskezaymwah, voo pahrlay ahnglay?

Excuse me, is this the right way to the port/the city centre/ the tourist office/the station/the bus station?
Excusez-moi, c'est la bonne direction pour le vieux port/ le centre-ville/l'office de tourisme/la gare/la gare routière?
Ekskewzaymwah, seh lah bon deerekseeawng poor leh veeuh pohr/leh sahngtr veel/lohfeece de tooreezm/lah gahr/lah gahr rootyair?

Can you point to it on my map?
Pourriez-vous me le montrer sur la carte?
Pooreehvoo mer ler mawngtreh sewr lah kart?

Marseilles' main train station, Gare Saint-Charles. A one-way ticket costs €8.50, and the journey takes about 25 minutes. The main bus station, or gare routière, is located just behind the Gare Saint-Charles ⓐ rue Honnorat, pl. Victor Hugo ☎ 08 91 02 40 25 🌐 www.infociao.com Ⓜ Metro: 1, 2 to St-Charles
Transport Routier Passagers Aeriens (TRPA) ☎ 04 91 50 59 34 🌐 www.infociao.com

To get in to the city centre from the A7 motorway or the airport by car, take the A55 in the direction of the Vieux Port. Alternatively, if you're arriving from the south, take the corniche John Fitzgerald

Marseilles

0 ——— 500 metres
0 ——— 500 yards

Key
- POI
- Ⓜ Metro Stop
- ✝ Cathedral
- ⓘ Information
- Police Station
- ✈ Airport
- Railway Stn
- Bus Station
- ✚ Hospital

N

Marseilles-Provence ✈
PLACE DE LA JOLIETTE
Joliette Ⓜ
RUE DU MONT LIBAN
RUE ISMAILY

Gare Maritimes-Internationales
BLVD DES DAMES
RUE DE LA RÉPUBLIQUE

Bassin de la Grand Joliette
L'AUTOROUTE DU LITTORAL
BOULEVARD DE DUNKERQUE

Cathédrale de la Major ✝
Vieille Charité
RUE DE L'EVÊCHÉ
RUE DE LA LOGE
2e ARR
PLACE SADI CARNOT

AVE VAUDOYER
RUE DES MUETS
Eglise St-Laurent
Musée des Docks Romains
Théâtre Grec
Hôtel de Ville

Fort Saint Jean
QUAI DU PORT
Vieux Port Ⓜ

Palais du Pharo
Vieux Port

Château d'If
Centre Nautique Marseilles
Parc du Pharo
Bas Fort Saint-Nicolas
Bassin de Carenage

Les Catalans Beach
BOULEVARD CHARLES LIVON
QUAI DE RIVE NEUVE
PLACE AUX HUILES

R. DE SUEZ
RUE DE SUEZ
AVENUE PASTEUR
Théâtre National
RUE STE-CATHERINE
RUE SAINTE

CHARLES ALEMAN
Fort Saint-Nicolas
SAINTE
St Victor Abbey
BOULEVARD DE LA CORDERIE

Monument aux Morts des Armées d'Orient
CORNICHE PRES. J KENNEDY
RUE DES CATALAN
AVE DE LA CORSE
AVENUE DE LA CORSE
PLACE DU 18 SEPTEMBRE
Jardin P Puget
COURS
Institut des Sourds-Muets et Aveugles

RUE AUGUSTIN
RUE DE SAMATIN
RUE PAUL BROCA
CODACCIONI
SAUVEUR
TOBELEM
Notre-Dame de la Garde

7e ARR
RUE DES COTEAUX D'ENDOURME
RUE PERLET
AVE DU ROI RENE

Théâtre Sylvain
Monument des Rapatriés d'Algérie
Parc Montvert
BOULEVARD DES FLOTS BLEUS

52

Kennedy. If you are not used to driving in continental Europe, note that it's necessary to be very assertive, especially in traffic. Leave your car at one of the 15 city car parks as soon as possible: the city is much easier to navigate on foot or by public transport.

Parking Bourse (ⓐ Centre Bourse, rue Reine Elisabeth ⓘ 04 91 91 19 23), **Parking De Gaulle** (ⓐ pl. du General de Galle ⓘ 04 91 33 97 24) and **Parking Vieux Port** (ⓐ cours d'Estienne d'Orves ⓘ 04 91 54 34 38) are all centrally located.

By water

Ferries arrive at the **Ferry Port** (ⓐ 61 blvd des Dames ⓘ 3260 ⓦ www.sncm.fr Ⓝ Metro: 2 to Joliette) from Corsica, Sardinia, Tunisia and Algeria.

◗ *The new tramway makes navigation of the city even easier*

FINDING YOUR FEET

Take the time to get to know the various areas of the city.
The Marseillaise are a tolerant lot so don't be shy about asking
directions. It's better to avoid quiet and poorly lit areas at night,
and always keep an eye on your belongings.

ORIENTATION

Exiting the Saint-Charles train station, the entire city is at
your feet. Head down to La Canebière, the long street leading
from east to west, directly to the quai des Belges in the Vieux
Port. The Panier district is to the north of the port, while the
Palais du Pharo and Notre-Dame are to the south. Les Catalans
beach is a ten-minute walk from the Vieux Port, heading
south along the coast. Hop on a sightseeing bus tour or
the Petit-Train (see page 24 for details of both) to get your
bearings. Walking tours are also organised by the tourist
office (see page 137).

The maps in this guide are up to date and show all the main
sights and streets in each area, but many of the places that we
list are on smaller streets. If you are planning to stay in Marseilles
for longer than a couple of days, it's a good idea to acquire
a detailed map locally.

GETTING AROUND

Marseilles' city centre and Vieux Port are easily walkable, and the
narrow roads of the Panier district are best explored on foot.

The **Marseilles Transit Authority** (**RTM** Ⓦ www.rtm.fr) operates
bus lines covering the entire city centre and the suburbs, and
including transport to nearby towns. Buses run from 05.00–21.00.

Aéroport
Marseille-Provence ✈

Paris, Montpellier
& Nîmes

Aix-en-Provence

Sèptemes

①
La Rose
*Technopole de
Château-Gombert*

Ste Marthe

Frais Vallon

Marseille
Saint-Charles

Malpassé

Saint Just
Hôtel du Département

Chartreux

National   Longchamp

Canebière
Garibaldi

Réformés -
Canebière

Cinq Avenues -
Longchamp

Cinq Avenues

Noailles Ⓣ①

Foch Sakakini

Ⓣ②
Blancarde
Foch

Eugène Pierre

Foch Boisson

Marseille
Blancarde

Camas   George   Jean
Martin

Blancarde
Chave

Sainte Thérèse

Saint Pierre

Notre Dame du Mont
Cours Julien

①
La Timone

La Parette

Les Caillols Ⓣ①

Castellane   Baille

La Pomme

Périer

Rond-Point
du Prado

Ste Marguerite - Dromel ②

Cannes, Antibes, Nice

Nightbuses ('Fluobus') cover some of the routes between 21.00 and 05.00.

Marseilles has two metro lines (1 & 2, blue and red respectively). Line 1 serves La Fourragère to La Rose, while line 2 serves Sainte-Marguerite/Dromel to Bougainville. The metro runs from 05.00–21.00 Mon–Thur, and 05.00–00.30 Fri–Sun.

Marseilles' first tramway opened at the end of June 2007 and by the autumn of 2007, both T1 (Les Caillols to Eugène Pierre) and T2 (Blancarde Foch to Euroméditerranée Gantès) were operational (ⓦ www.le-tram.fr).

All tickets for public transport are valid for buses, the metro or the tram. A single ticket ('Solo', €1.70) is good for one hour. A Carte Journée (€4.50) is good for one day of travel on public transport, while a seven-day pass costs €10.60. For further information about all public transport ❶ 04 91 91 92 10 ⓦ www.lepilote.com

In the centre of the city, taxis are easy to find. Your hotel or more upmarket restaurants and bars can call a taxi for you; otherwise try **Taxi Radio Marseilles** ❶ 04 91 02 20 20 or **Taxi Blanc Bleu** ❶ 04 91 03 60 03

CAR HIRE

The best spots to pick up hire cars are at the airport or at the Gare Saint-Charles. It's worth booking a car ahead of time, as on-the-spot deals are rarely deals at all.

Avis (Gare Saint-Charles) ❶ 08 20 61 16 36
Budget (Airport) ❶ 08 25 00 35 64
Hertz (Airport) ❶ 08 25 09 13 13

▶ *Marseilles' skyline stretches as far as the eye can see*

THE CITY OF
Marseilles

Vieux Port & Le Panier

The Vieux Port (Old Port) is the historical heart of Marseilles, where the original city was born and developed. Now the second-largest pleasure harbour in Europe, restaurants and cafés line the quays, and regular ferry services depart from the quai des Belges to the Ile d'If and the Calanques. Le Panier, or 'the breadbasket' (named for the prolific Greek market that used to exist here), is Marseilles' medieval quarter, sitting snugly to the north of the port. A Greek temple originally graced place des Moulins, the highest hilltop in the district, and the same site was later home to 15 windmills, giving the place its name. (Two remain, but have been converted to private homes.) During World War II, Jewish families and Resistance fighters sought refuge in the quarter's unmapped streets, and parts of the district were later evacuated and bombed by the Nazis. In the 1970s Le Panier earned a name for itself as a gritty heroin den, most of which was eventually exported to the US. Over the last decade, affluent buyers have begun to snap up the charming townhouses that line the traffic-free alleys, and the quarter is slowly undergoing a massive gentrification.

SIGHTS & ATTRACTIONS

Cathédrale de la Major

Built in the 19th century, this Romano-Byzantine style cathedral was modelled on Saint Sophia Church in Istanbul. It is the largest cathedral built in France since the Middle Ages, although it's never been as popular as Marseilles' Bonne Mère (see page 95). Check

⬥ *The imposing façade of the 19th-century Cathédrale de la Major*

THE CITY

Vieux Port & Le Panier

	POI
M	Metro Stop
	Cathedral
i	Information
	Police Station
	Airport
	Railway Stn
	Bus Station
	Hospital

N

PLACE DE LA JOLIETTE

RUE DE FORBIN

Joliette M

RUE DE PLUMIER

RUE D'HOCTER

QUAI JEAN CHARCOT

Bassin de la Grand Joliette

Gare Maritimes-Internationales

La Joliette

BOULEVARD DE DUNKERQUE

BOULEVARD DES DAMES

RUE JEAN-FRANÇOIS LECA

Vieille Charité (Musée d'Archéologie Mediteranéenne, Musée d'Arts Africains, Oceaniens et Amérindiens)

RUE DE LA RÉPUBLIQUE

Cathédrale de la Major

RUE DES PETITS PUITS

RUE DU PANIER

PL SADI CARNOT

TERRE PLAIN DE LA TOURETTE

AVE VAUDOYER

2e ARR

PLACE DES GRAND RUE AUGUSTINES

Château d'If

Eglise Saint-Laurent

Fort Saint Jean

RUE CAISSERIE

Musé des Docks Romains

Musée du Vieux Marseille

Théâtre Grec

RUE DE LA LOGE

QUAI DU PORT

Hôtel de Ville

Palais du Pharo

Parc du Pharo

Port de la Réserve

Club Nautique Marseillais

Bas Fort Saint-Nicolas

Vieux Port

BOULEVARD CHARLES LIVON

Bassin de Carenage

QUAI DE RIVE NEUVE

PLACE AUX HUILES

Théâtre National

COURS D'ESTIE D'ORV

RUE DE SUEZ

AVENUE PASTEUR

RUE PAPETY

Fort Saint-Nicolas

RUE SAINTE

SAINTE-CATHERINE

RUE C ALEMAN

RUE GIRADIN

LE PHARO

Saint Victor Abbey

7e ARR

TUNNEL P CARENAGE

CORDERIE

BOULEVARD DE LA

62

> ### THE RHINO OF THE ILE D'IF
> Bizarrely, in 1516 the Ile d'If was temporarily home to
> a rhinoceros, a gift on its way from the King of Portugal to
> Pope Leo X. The Marseillaise were enamoured, and turned
> out in droves to admire the creature and smother it with
> love. Unfortunately, this clearly softened the little fellow
> up as it died just off the coast of Genoa, before it reached
> its final destination.

with the tourist office for a schedule of the cathedral's organ
concerts. Ⓜ Metro: 2 to Joliette; bus: 55, 83

Château d'If
In 1524 King François I built this fortress, which was used as
a prison soon after, in order to protect the city from invasion by
sea. The island and the château owe much of their international
fame to author Alexandre Dumas, who imprisoned his fictitious
character Edmond Dantès here in *The Count of Monte Cristo*. To
visit the château, hop on the 20-minute ferry from quai des Belges
(€10 return). ⓐ Ile d'If ☎ 04 91 59 02 30 🕐 09.00–18.30 Tues–Sun,
June–Aug; 09.00–18.00 Tues–Sun, Sept–May. Admission charge

Eglise Saint-Laurent
The only building left standing when Nazis evacuated and bombed
the entire district in Feb 1943, this church is now surrounded by
1950s housing blocks. ⓐ Esplanade de la Tourette ☎ 04 91 90 52 87
🕐 Masses only Ⓜ Bus: 55, 83

Fort Saint Jean

A second military fort, again by Louis XIV, which was built in order to ensure total control over Marseilles' Port. The Museum of European and Mediterranean Civilizations is now located here. 🚍 Bus: 55, 83

Fort Saint-Nicolas

Located between Saint-Victor Abbey and the Pharo, Fort Saint-Nicolas was built by Louis XIV to defend Marseilles. However, he also installed a line of canons pointed toward shore, to keep local citizens under control, as he was never entirely convinced of their loyalty. 🚍 Bus: 83

🔺 *Château d'If, site of the fictitious Count of Monte Cristo*

Frioul islands

Second stop on the same ferries that service the Château d'If, the Frioul islands are a popular destination for fishing or lazing on the beach. They were formerly a quarantine port and site of the Caroline Hospital. Head away from the crowds to explore the islands' natural beauty and indigenous species. The new port, which was designed in 1974, is somewhat lacking in character. ❶ 04 91 46 54 65 🅝 Boats to the Ile d'If and the Frioul islands depart from the Vieux Port, quai de la Fraternité

Hôtel de Ville (City Hall)

Architects Gaspard Puget and Mathieu Portal designed the Genoese-influenced City Hall located on the quai du Port. For the best view of this building, take the César ferryboat from the Place aux Huiles across the Vieux Port, descending in front of the City Hall. (single €0.50, return €0.80) 🅝 Metro: 1 to Vieux-Port; bus: 83

La Joliette

Head down rue de la Republique to La Joliette, the city's 19th-century hub for port activities. In 1858, Marseilles' Docks and Warehouse Company built the four brick and stone buildings known as the Joliette Docks, largest in the world at the time. The buildings were designed by Gustave Desplaces and were inspired by the London Docks. Now part of the Euroméditerranée project (see page 16), the buildings have been renovated by architect Eric Castaldi. 🅝 Metro: 2 to Joliette; tram: 1 to Joliette; bus: 55, 83

● *The Joliette Docks have given new life to the surrounding area*

Archways and windows face a central courtyard at La Vieille Charité

La Vieille Charité

Built during 17th and 18th centuries, this enormous complex was originally home for the ill and poor. Keeping with the style of the times, all windows faced an interior courtyard, so as not to offend passers by. Pierre Puget, the celebrated local architect, designed the courtyard's baroque Oval Chapel. Plans to raze the entire building were afoot iduring 1940s, but Le Corbusier worked to get it listed as local monument. It is currently home to two museums, and regular courses for adults, school groups and children are organised here. ⓐ 2 rue de la Vieille-Charité ⓘ 04 91 14 58 80 Ⓜ Metro: 2 to Joliette; tram: 1 to Republique-Dames; bus: 55, 83

CULTURE

Musée d'Archéologie Méditerranéenne
(Mediterranean Archaeology Museum)

With the second-largest Egyptian collection in France (following the Louvre), this museum contains a wide variety of archaeological artefacts from Marseilles through to the Middle East.
ⓐ La Vieille Charité, 2 rue de la Vieille-Charité ⓛ 11.00–18.00 Tues–Sun, June–Sept; 10.00–17.00 Tues–Sun, Oct–May, closed Mon ⓝ Metro: 2 to Joliette; tram: 1 to Republique-Dames; bus: 55, 83. Admission charge

Musée d'Arts Africains, Océaniens et Amérindiens
(Museum of African, Oceanic and American Indian Art)

Both a permanent collection of traditional international artworks and a temporary exhibition space, this museum is also hosting rotating exhibitions from the Musée des Beaux-Arts (closed for renovations until 2010). ⓐ La Vieille Charité, 2 rue de la Vieille-Charité ⓛ 11.00–18.00 Tues–Sun, June–Sept; 10.00–17.00 Tues–Sun, Oct–May, closed Mon ⓝ Metro: 2 to Joliette; tram: 1 to Republique-Dames; bus: 55, 83. Admission charge

Musée des Docks Romains (Roman Docks Museum)

Items retrieved from sunken ships off Marseilles' coast are displayed alongside information relating to the city's nautical history from 600 BC to AD 400. ⓐ pl. Vivaux ⓣ 04 91 91 24 62 ⓛ 11.00–18.00 Tues–Sun, June–Sept; 10.00–17.00 Tues–Sun, Oct–May, closed Mon ⓝ Métro: Vieux-Port. Admission charge

Musée du Vieux Marseille (Museum of Old Marseilles)
Temporary exhibitions give a good overview of how the city's
traditions, such as the dance of the 'Balade le nez en l'air', and
popular culture have developed over the centuries. ⓐ Maison
Diamantée, 2 rue de la Prison ⓣ 04 91 55 28 68 ⓛ 10.00–17.00
Tues–Sun, Oct–May; 11.00–18.00 Tues–Sun, June–Sept, closed Mon
ⓝ Métro: Vieux-Port; bus: 83, 49B. Admission charge

RETAIL THERAPY

Des Anées Lumières Wildly imaginative chandeliers and light
fixtures are decorated with faux flowers, fruits and crystals.

MARSEILLES' MARKETABILITY
You can't go wrong with a visit to a local market. Apart from
the sometimes unique purchases you can make, these are
great places to plug into the real vibe of the city and watch
its inhabitants go about their business. Marseilles is rich in
market life, of which the following three are among the most
vivacious. If you're into fresh, much of the produce on sale
at the Fish Market on quai des Belges has been caught just
off the coast of the nearby Calanques. For breadth of choice
in a part of the city that's buzzing right now, you should head
immediately for place de la Joliette's Produce Market. Antiques
lovers will adore the Brocante Market at avenue du Cap
Pinède where a mixture of vintage and second-hand items
offer the (sometimes false) promise of a tidy little profit.

ⓐ 365 ave Mazargues ⓣ 06 75 10 54 08 ⓔ veronique.sarafian@free.fr
ⓛ 10.00–13.00, 14.30–19.00 Mon–Sat ⓝ Tram: 1 to Republique-Dames

La Bastide des Bains Spoil yourself with a winter warmer at
La Bastide's hammam. Primarily female only, there are also
mixed bathing sessions (swimming costume obligatory) four
times a week. ⓐ 19 rue Sainte ⓣ 04 91 33 39 13 ⓦ www.bastide-
des-bains.com ⓛ 10.00–20.30 Mon & Wed, 10.00–20.00 Tues
& Thur, Fri & Sat, 09.00–14.00 Sun ⓝ Metro: 1 to Vieux-Port

La Chocolatière du Panier
The Le Ray family have been
creating their own delicious
chocolates according to
family recipes for three
generations now. ⓐ 4 pl. des
13 Cantons ⓣ 04 91 91 67 66
ⓛ 09.00–13.00, 14.30–19.00
Mon–Sat ⓝ Tram: 1 to
Republique-Dames

Manon Martin Order the
hat of your dreams, made
to measure, at renowned
Marseillaise milliner Manon
Martin. ⓐ 10 rue de la Tour

⬤ *The eccentric 1920s storefront
of La Chocolatière du Panier*

ⓣ 04 91 55 60 95 ⓛ 10.00–19.00 Tues–Sat, 14.00–19.00 Mon
ⓝ Metro: 1 to Estrangin; bus: 61, 80

TAKING A BREAK

Like any big city, Marseilles can occasionally necessitate a bit of feet-up time. The ultimately relaxed vibe on which it runs means that it's easy to find somewhere sympathetic to those who want to chill before paying the bill.

Le Bar de la Marine £ ❶ The site of Marcel Pagnol's trilogy, *Marius, Fanny,* and *César,* this port-side bar was also featured in the film *Love Actually.* Enjoy a *pastis* among the old photos and nautical murals. ⓐ 15 quai de Rive Neuve ❶ 04 91 54 95 42 🕐 07.00–24.00 Ⓝ Metro: 1 to Vieux-Port

Cafés Debout £ ❷ For outstanding freshly ground coffee and friendly service, head to Cafés Debout, in business since 1932. ⓐ 46 rue Francis-Davso ❶ 04 91 33 00 12 Ⓦ www.cafesdebout.com 🕐 08.00–19.00 Mon–Sat Ⓝ Metro: 1 to Vieux-Port

L'Effet Clochette £ ❸ Tables litter the terrace in front of this corner café. Go for the home-made chips, and pick up some unusual jewellery. ⓐ 2 pl. des Augustines ❶ 04 91 90 15 75 🕐 10.00–18.00 Ⓝ Tram: 1 to Republique-Dames

Le Treize Coins £ ❹ Featured in local author Izzo's detective novels, this little bar has cleaned up its reputation in recent years. Go for the sawdust on the floors and the outstanding tagines. ⓐ 45 rue Sainte-Françoise ❶ 04 91 90 43 27 🕐 08.00–22.00 Ⓝ Tram: 1 to Republique-Dames

Vitalifruit £ 5 Feed your body liquid health, in the form
of fresh-squeezed juices and smoothies, at Vitalifruit.
Stop by near closing time to pick up half-price sandwiches.
🅐 11A cours Estienne d'Orves 🕿 04 91 54 82 18 🕒 09.00–19.00
�metro Metro: 1 to Vieux-Port

Café Parisien ££ 6 Utterly French, Café Parisien is good for
breakfast or a light lunch. Alternatively, order an aperitif and
visit their *boulodrome*, hidden *boules* pitch (free with drink).
🅐 1 pl. Sadi Carnot 🕿 04 91 90 05 77 🕒 08.00–16.00 Mon, Tues
& Thurs–Sun, 08.00–01.00 Wed � Tram: 1 to Sadi-Carnot

La Caravelle ££ 7 Located on the first floor of the Hotel Belle Vue,
go between 18.00–21.00 for plate after plate of scrumptious (free)
snacks with your drink. Décor: oh, so French. 🅐 34 quai du Port
🕿 04 91 90 36 64 🕒 08.00–02.00 �metro Metro: 1 to Vieux-Port

AFTER DARK

RESTAURANTS

Le 504 £ 8 Boasts the best Tunisian tagines on the Vieux Port.
🅐 34 pl. aux Huiles 🕿 04 91 33 57 74 🕒 Lunch & dinner Mon–Sat,
closed Sun �metro Metro: 1 to Vieux-Port

Heng-Heng £ 9 Utterly simple, with its long white tables and
no-frills décor, this Vietnamese restaurant is a local favourite.
Outstanding. 🅐 65 rue de la Republique 🕒 12.00–23.00 Wed–Mon,
closed Tues � Tram: 1 to Republique-Dames

La Karbonade £ ❿ Meats (including *andouillette*, or blood sausage) and grills are the speciality at this vibrant restaurant on the Vieux Port. Entrées and desserts can be ordered in *degustation* (smaller tasting) portions. ⓐ 42 quai de Rive-Neuve ⓣ 04 91 55 02 27 ⓦ www.lakarbonade.com ⓛ Lunch & dinner Mon–Sat, closed Sun ⓝ Bus: 83

Lemon Grass ££ ⓫ Just around the corner from the Place aux Huiles, Lemongrass's modern French cuisine is mouth-watering. Try the lobster ravioli. ⓐ 8 rue Fort-Notre-Dame ⓣ 04 91 33 97 65 ⓛ Lunch & dinner Tues–Fri, Dinner Sat, closed Sun ⓝ Metro: 1 to Vieux-Port; bus: 55, 57, 60, 81, 83

La Virgule ££ ⓬ Modern takes on 1970s classics, like egg mayonnaise. In a rush? Order the €19 Apostrophe menu (lunch only) – it's served in under 20 minutes at the counter. ⓐ 27 rue de la Loge ⓣ 04 91 90 91 11 ⓛ Lunch & dinner ⓝ Metro: 1 to Vieux-Port; bus: 83

Miramar £££ ⓭ Owned by the Minguella brothers, Miramar serves the best *bouillabaisse* on the Vieux Port, at a price to match. ⓐ 12 quai du Port ⓣ 04 91 91 10 40 ⓛ Lunch & dinner, Tues–Sat, closed Sun & Mon ⓝ Metro: 1 to Vieux-Port

BARS & CLUBS

Pêle-Mêle An excellent spot to stop for an aperitif, a nightcap, or to check out the awesome live jazz. ⓐ 8 pl. aux Huiles ⓣ 04 91 54 85 26 ⓛ 19.00–02.00 Tues–Sat, closed Sun & Mon ⓝ Metro: 1 to Vieux-Port

Le Trolleybus Music to suit everyone's taste, depending on the night. Le Trolleybus has been one of the most popular clubs in Marseilles for years. ⓐ 24 quai de Rive Neuve ⓦ letrolley.com ⓛ 23.00–06.00 Tues–Sat, closed Sun & Mon ⓝ Metro: 1 to Vieux-Port; bus: 55, 57, 60, 81, 83

ARTS & ENTERTAINMENT

La Criée Between 1975 and 1981, the city's former fish market was renovated and changed into an outstanding theatre. ⓣ 04 91 54 70 54 ⓦ www.theatre-lacriee.com ⓛ closed Aug

● As night falls, diners begin to fill restaurant terraces in city squares

The city centre

Marseilles' downtown area centres primarily around La Canebière, the city's central artery. Taking its name from *canebe*, or the hemp rope produced by factories that used to be located close to the shipyards, La Canebière stretches from the Réformés metro stop down to the Vieux Port. The modern tramline travels almost its entire length, providing easy access to shops and museums. While its glory is somewhat faded, La Canebière is due to be spruced up as part of the city's urban renewal project.

The enthusiastic shopper can dedicate days to this area, starting at the Porte d'Aix, heading down cours Belsunce and the rue de Rome. International high-street stores, like H&M and Virgin, can be found on rue Saint-Ferréol, while top designers are located on many of the smaller cross streets, like rue Grignan and rue de la Tour.

Cours Julien and Le Plaine are the place to go for a dose of urban counter culture. Stop at one of the cafés spilling out under plane trees, shop at the weekly organic market or pick up offbeat albums or books here. Restaurants span the globe with their cuisines.

SIGHTS & ATTRACTIONS

Palais de la Bourse (Stock Exchange)

Home to the oldest Chamber of Commerce in France (founded in 1599) and the Musée de la Maritine et de l'Economie (Maritime and Economy Museum), the Palais de la Bourse was built and

⬤ *Fountains along the pedestrianised cours Julien*

inaugurated under Napoleon III. La Canebière Museum 10.00–18.00 Metro: 1 to Vieux-Port. Admission charge

Parc et Palais de Longchamp (Longchamp Park and Palace)

This incredible structure and the surrounding gardens were built over 11 years by 5,000 workers, directed by Espérandieu and completed in the mid-19th century. The project was initiated after the drought of 1834, when it was decided that drastic means must be taken in order to ensure the safe storage of water reserves. A water tower stands at the centre of the Palais, and is flanked by the Musée des Beaux-Arts (Fine Art Museum, closed for renovations until 2010) and the Musée d'Histoire Naturelle (Natural History Museum). Metro: 1 to Cinq-Avenues; tram: 1 to Longchamp, Cinq-Avenues; bus: 81

Porte d'Aix

Built in the 19th century, this old city gate leads out of Marseilles in the direction of Aix-en-Provence. It was added to the north end of the cours Belsunce, formerly one of the city's vast carriageways. Metro: 2 to Jules Guesde

CULTURE

Bibliothèque de l'Alcazar (Alcazar Municipal Library)

Formerly a theatre and music hall where Charlie Chaplin, among many others, performed, the Bibliothèque de l'Alcazar opened as a public library in 2004, following a six-year renovation project. It currently stages exhibitions and films, and is the second-largest library in France. 58 cours Belsunce 04 91 55 90 00

⬧ *The ornate Palais de Longchamp offers amazing views over the city*

🔺 *The ancient gardens contrast with surrounding modern architecture*

ⓦ www.bmvr.marseilles.fr 🕐 11.00–19.00 Tues–Sat, closed Sun & Mon ⓝ Tram: 1 to Belsunce

Jardins des Vestiges

These city ramparts and part of the ancient Roman port were discovered during the 1967 building of the Centre Bourse shopping centre. 🕐 04 91 90 42 22 🕐 12.00–19.00 Mon–Sat ⓝ Metro: 1 to Vieux-Port. Admission charge

Musée Cantini

A fantastic collection of modern and contemporary art, including artworks by Picasso, Signac, Giacometti and Bacon, located in a 17th-century mansion. ⓐ 19 rue Grignan ⓣ 04 91 54 77 75 ⓛ 10.00–17.00 Tues–Sun, Oct–May; 11.00–18.00 Tues–Sun, June–Sept, closed Mon ⓜ Métro: Estrangin; Bus: 21, 41, Admission charge

Musée Grobet-Labadie

This 19th-century family home, just opposite the Palais de Longchamp, has been preserved in all its splendour. Wander around the ten rooms to get a feel for turn-of-the-century bourgeois culture. ⓐ 140 blvd Longchamp ⓣ 04 91 62 21 82 ⓛ 11.00–18.00 Tues–Sun, June–Sept; 10.00–17.00 Tues–Sun, Oct–May ⓜ Metro: 1 to Cinq Avenues; tram: 1 to Longchamp; bus: 81

Musée d'Histoire Naturelle (Natural History Museum)

Located in a wing of the Palais de Longchamp, the Musée d'Histoire Naturelle offers examples of worldwide species, as well as a room dedicated to Provençal specimens. ⓐ Palais de Longchamp ⓣ 04 91 14 59 50 ⓛ 11.00–18.00 Tues–Sun, June–Sept; 10.00–17.00 Tues–Sun, Oct–May, closed Mon ⓜ Metro: 1 to Cinq Avenues; tram: 1 to Longchamp; bus: 81

Musée de la Mode (Fashion Museum)

A popular museum dedicated entirely to fashion. Be sure to pick up a flyer on the way in, as it contains necessary explanations about the exhibitions. ⓐ 11 La Canebière ⓣ 04 96 17 06 00 ⓛ 11.00–18.00 Tues–Sun, June–Sept; 10.00–17.00 Tues–Sun, Oct–May ⓜ Métro: Vieux-Port. Admission charge

Opera House

Rebuilt in 1919 after a fire destroyed almost the entire original 1787 building, Marseilles' Opera House stages a vivacious selection of opera and ballet throughout the year. ⓐ 2 rue Molière
ⓣ 04 91 55 14 99 Ⓜ Metro: 1 to Vieux-Port

RETAIL THERAPY

Marseilles Collections Shops in the city's Antiques District sell everything from high-priced collectibles to quirky purchases. Stop by this shop for a fine mix, including old postcards, toys, letters and documents. ⓐ 5 rue Edmond Rostand ⓣ 04 91 37 59 58
ⓞ 09.30–12.30, 14.00–18.30 Mon–Fri; 10.00–12.00, 14.00–17.30 Sat, closed Sun Ⓜ Metro: 1 to Estrangin, Castellane

MARKETS FOR FOODIES

Those who eschew a breakfast of fried bread, sausages and chips in favour of a more healthy bowl of muesli will find that central Marseilles has two markets selling fare whose wholesome munchability will test even the most omnivorous molars. The Marché des Capucins on place Capucin has a fantastically wide choice of nuts, vegetables and North African specialities. On Wednesday in the cours Julien, the Organic Market will allow you to fill your basket without so much as a passing care for pesticides or freeze-drying.

GARLIC GALORE
Between mid-June and mid-July, head up to the Garlic and
Taraïettes Fair on cours Belsunce. Provençal garlic is sold
in long braids, alongside *taraïettes*, which are enamelled
clay objects.

Oogie Opened by three friends from Marseilles, Oogie calls itself
a 'life store', and includes a boutique, hair salon and restaurant.
The place to shop for unusual music and art books. ⓐ 55 cours
Julien ⓣ 04 91 53 10 70 ⓦ www.myspace.com/oogielifestore
ⓛ Boutik 10.00–19.00 Mon–Sat, Brasserie 08.30–19.00 Mon–Wed,
Fri & Sat, 08.30–21.00 Thur ⓝ Metro: 2 to Notre-Dame du Mont;
bus: 74

Les Pipelettes Locally designed clothes for mothers-to-be and
children. The store also stocks a fantastic range of tote bags,
printed with local maps or Russian dolls. ⓐ 3 rue St Saëns
ⓣ 04 91 54 72 36 ⓛ 10.00–19.00 Mon–Sat, closed Sun
ⓝ Metro: 1 to Vieux-Port; bus: 61, 80

Savonnerie de la Licorne Owner Serge Bruna learned the art
of soap making from his grandfather, and everything in this
little factory is made according to traditional methods. Stop
in for a free tour of the site. ⓐ 34 cours Julien ⓣ 04 96 12 00 91
ⓛ 08.00–18.00 Mon–Fri, 10.00–18.00 Sat ⓝ Metro: 2 to Notre-
Dame du Mont; bus: 74

TAKING A BREAK

Dubble £ ❶ For soups, salads and healthy breakfast menus from
€4.20 (freshly squeezed juice, coffee and a muffin) stop by Dubble.
ⓐ 25 rue Sainte ❶ 04 91 90 37 98 ⓦ www.dubble-food.com
🕓 09.00–18.00 Mon–Sat, closed Sun, Aug Ⓜ Metro: 1 to
Vieux-Port; bus: 55

Eating 'pique-nique en ville' £ ❷ Pick up an outstanding sandwich
or take a break from shopping to enjoy one of the freshly made
salads at this cosy café. ⓐ 40 rue Montgrand ❶ 04 91 33 76 88
🕓 11.00–16.00 Mon–Sat, closed Sun Ⓜ Metro: 1 to Vieux-Port;
bus: 61, 80

Les Filles... du Soleil Gourmand £ ❸ Choose from a myriad of teas
in glass canisters, or go for one of the tasty daily light snacks. The
onsite store also sells quirky knick-knacks, like notebooks printed
with old French travel posters. ⓐ 71 cours Julien ❶ 04 91 92 53 76
🕓 10.00–19.00 Tues–Sat, closed Sun & Mon Ⓜ Metro: 2 to Notre-
Dame du Mont; bus: 74

Brasserie La Folle Epoque ££ ❹ Stop for an ice cream or an aperitif
under the wide umbrellas of this pavement café. Be sure to check
out the old photographs and the antique copper coffee machine
inside. ⓐ 10 pl. Felix Baret ❶ 04 91 33 38 24 🕓 08.00–21.00
Ⓜ Metro: 1 to Estrangin

▶ *While away the afternoon with a coffee in place Felix Baret*

AFTER DARK

RESTAURANTS

La Jardin d'à Côte £ A fun, inexpensive spot favoured by Marseilles' young crowd. Try the *Assiette Marseillaise* (Marseilles plate) for a little taste of their specialities. ⓐ 65 cours Julien ⓣ 04 91 94 15 51 ⓛ Lunch & dinner Mon–Sat, June–Sept, Lunch Mon–Sat, Oct–May Ⓝ Metro: 2 to Notre-Dame du Mont; bus: 74

Le Carbone ££ Enjoy French cuisine with Asian highlights, while listening to jazzy music and checking out the retro décor. At lunch, try the excellent-value €14 menu. ⓐ 22 rue Sainte ⓣ 04 91 55 52 73 ⓛ Lunch Mon–Sat, Dinner Tues–Sat, closed Sun, Aug Ⓝ Metro: 1 to Vieux-Port; bus: 55

La Patte de l'Ours ££ With a menu favouring organic produce and based entirely on seasonal specialties, this little gem is a fine balance between upmarket restaurant and healthy cuisine. Finish off your meal with one of their fabulous international coffee blends. ⓐ 4 pl. Cézanne ⓣ 06 21 52 49 20 ⓛ 08.00–18.00 Tues & Wed, 08.00–22.00 Thur–Sat, 08.00–15.00 Sun, closed Mon & Aug Ⓝ Metro: 2 to Notre-Dame du Mont; bus: 74

Le Resto Provençal ££ The funky décor and checkerboard floors set the stage for tasty recipes from the region. ⓐ 64 cours Julien ⓣ 04 91 48 85 12 ⓛ 12.00–14.00 Tues–Fri, 20.00–22.30 Tues–Sat, closed Sun & Mon Ⓝ Metro: 2 to Notre-Dame du Mont; bus: 74

Toinou Coquillages ££ ❾ A Marseillaise institution, this seafood spot has been in business for over 40 years. Fancy oysters on the beach? Buy seafood to take away from their stand too. ⓐ 18 cours St Louis (off La Canebière) ⓣ 04 91 54 08 79 ⓦ www.toinou.com ⓛ Lunch & dinner, no reservations ⓝ Metro: 2 to Noailles

BARS & CLUBS

New Cancan One of the most popular gay clubs in Marseilles. ⓐ 3–7 rue Sénac ⓣ 04 91 48 59 76 ⓦ www.newcancan.com ⓛ 23.00–dawn Thur–Sun ⓝ Metro: 2 to Noailles

ARTS & ENTERTAINMENT

Espace Julien For theatre, comedy and live music, check out the weekly happenings at Espace Julien. ⓐ 39 cours Julien ⓣ 04 91 24 34 10 ⓦ www.espace-julien.com ⓝ Metro: 2 to Notre-Dame du Mont; bus: 74

La Friche de la Belle de Mai Located in a former tobacco factory, La Friche stages everything from exhibitions and theatre to gastronomic events and concerts. Constantly in flux, days could be whiled away in this massive complex. ⓐ 41 rue Jobin ⓣ 04 95 04 95 04 ⓦ www.lafriche.org ⓛ mostly closed in Aug ⓝ Bus: 33, 34, 49

South of the Port

Marseilles sprawls southward from the Vieux Port. Neighbourhoods fluctuate from the tangle of streets just behind quai de Rive Neuve to the spacious avenue du Prado. An eclectic mix of restaurants, beaches and business centres, this area of Marseilles is the city's most varied, and is an appropriate reflection of its many facets.

SIGHTS & ATTRACTIONS

Avenue Prado

Often called Marseilles' Champs-Elysées, the avenue Prado is home to boutiques and business centres, while large shady trees spread over the daily market. Visit place Castellane, with its famous marble fountain built and donated to the city by Jules Cantini, and the Parc du 26ème Centaire (the 26th Century Park, also known as the Millennium Park). The latter was inaugurated in 2000 to celebrate the city's 2,600 years of history, and includes 26 sequoias (one for each century). ● Park 08.00–21.00 May–Aug; 08.00–19.00 Mar & Apr, Sept & Oct; 08.00–17.30 Nov–Feb ● Metro: Castellane, then bus: 18, 42, 50

Beaches

Public and private beaches line the coast, from **Les Catalans** (● Bus: 83), to the Prado beaches, created using land reclaimed from the building of the city's metro system in the 1970s, down to the **Pointe Rouge** (● Metro: Point-Rouge du Prado; bus: 19).

● The sand and shallow waters at Les Catalans beach are perfect for kids

South of the Port

0   500 metres
0   500 yards

Legend:
- POI
- Metro Stop
- Cathedral
- Information
- Police Station
- Airport
- Railway Stn
- Bus Station
- Hospital

Fort Saint Jean
Eglise St-Laurent
Théâtre Grec
Palais du Pharo
Parc du Pharo
Port de la Réserve
Bas Fort Saint-Nicolas
Centre Nautique Marseilles
Club Nautique Marseillais
ESPLANADE DU PHARO
BOULEVARD CHARLES LIVON
Bassin de Carenage
RAMPE SAINT-MAURICE
Château d'If
Les Catalans Beach
RUE DES CATALANS
RUE DE SUEZ
IMPASSE CERVILLE
AVENUE PASTEUR
Fort Saint-Nicolas
RUE PAPETY
RUE CESAR ALEMAN
RUE GIRADIN
ST NICOLAS
LE PHARO
Saint Victor Abbey
AVENUE DE LA CORSE
AVENUE DE LA CORSE
RUE FRANCOIS
Saint Sainte
CHARLES
RUE CAP DESSEMOND
PLACE DU 4 SEPTEMBRE
RUE HENRI VALER
RUE SOLILER
RUE OLIVE
RUE DU TOUR
A CHAUX
RUE DE LA CAZE
RUE DE NICE
RUE ST PAUL
CODACCIONI
RUE SAUVEUR TOBELEM
Monument aux Morts des Armées d'Orient
CORNICHE PRESIDENT JOHN KENNEDY
BOULEVARD DE LA PLAGE
BOULEVARD DES DARDANELLES
VALLON DES AUFFES
RUE JOUVE
RUE DE SAMIN
RUE FENELON et ROBERT GUICKEL
RUE DES VICCHINI
CHATEAUBRIANT
CHERKIS
RUE DES COTEAUX
TADREI
RUE D'ENDOURME
RUE DU VALLON DES AUFFES
RUE HENRI
VALLON DES AUFFES
RUE TURCON
RUE PERLET
DU ROI RENE
RUE DES PECHEURS
AVE E ORAISON
RUE DE CHATEAU D'IF
RUE PIERRE MOULEN
BOULEVARD D'ENDOURME
RUE D'ENDOURME
IMP DU RIF
BLVD DE TASA
IMP FOUQUE
TRAV DU FRIOUL
RUE RAPON
RUE CHANE
AVE E ETIENNE
BOULEVARD
RUE NICOLAS CACNEL
RUE MICHEL
RUE J AICARD
RUE DU DOCTEUR CANIER
BLVD MARIUS THOMAS
RUE FOREST
RUE RICAUD
IMP A AUTRAN
BOULEVARD A AUTRAN
7e ARR
Théâtre Sylvain
RUE DES PONS
CHEMIN
RUE DES FLOTS BLEUS
IMPASSE VERMER
BLVD BOMPARD
RUE ETIENNE MEIN
R M BRIGNADY
AVE DES ROCHES
Monument des Rapatriés d'Algérie
Parc Montvert

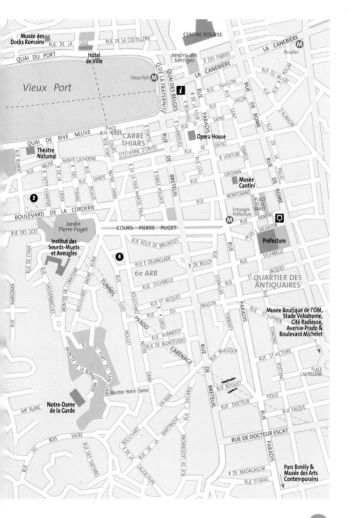

Near the Parc du Prado, there is one beach reserved solely for the use of windsurfers. Public beaches tend to be crowded – if you need a little more space, try La Paillote des Catalans (next door to Les Catalans). Entrance for the day is just €5.

Carré Thiars
Located just south of the Vieux Port (just off rue Sainte), this area was originally built by Louis XIV in order to house an arsenal of galleys. The project was never fully realised, and the abandoned warehouses and courtyards have now been taken over by a lively variety of restaurants, bars, galleries and theatres.
Ⓝ Metro: 1 to Vieux-Port

Cité Radieuse
This 'Radiant City' was designed by Swiss architect Charles-Edouard Jeanneret (Le Corbusier), and built between 1947 and 1952. Raoul Dautry, the city's post-war Minister of Reconstruction, employed Le Corbusier to assist in solving massive housing shortages. The result was this incredible futuristic housing complex, made up of 338 apartments on 18 floors.

IF YOU FANCY A LONG SIT DOWN...
According to the Guinness Book of World Records, the bench located on the corniche John Fitzgerald Kennedy is the longest in the world! Take Bus: 83 over from the quai des Belges in order to check it out, and while you're sprawled out on it, you'll be enthralled by the fine sea views.

Monument aux Morts des Armées d'Orient

The sculptor Sartorio created this monument, dedicated to fallen soldiers. Perfectly positioned on the JFK Corniche, visitors standing in front of the sculpture have a direct view of the Château d'If. Bus: 83

Monument des Rapatriés d'Algérie

Created by the contemporary artist César, this sculpture honours those who chose to settle in Marseilles after Algerian independence. ⓐ corniche John Fitzgerald Kennedy Ⓝ Bus: 83

Notre-Dame de la Garde ('La Bonne Mère')

Exiting the Gare Saint-Charles, this striking landmark will be the first sight that catches your gaze. Originally a 13th-century chapel, the prime location of the Notre-Dame de la Garde led François I to enlarge and fortify the church, for the protection of the city, during the 16th century. Modified and tweaked over the years, the enormous Romanesque-Byzantine basilica was completed by Espérandieu in the 19th century. The Notre-Dame de la Garde and its 10-m (33-ft) Virgin Mary (La Bonne Mère), are believed to protect local fishermen, and a procession to the church is made every 15 August. ⓐ pl. Colonel Edon ☏ 04 91 13 40 80 ⓦ www.notredamedelagarde.com ⏱ 07.00–19.00 June–Sept; 07.30–17.30 Oct–May Ⓝ Bus: 60 (also accessible by foot, Petit-Train and Le Grand Tour bus)

Parc et Palais du Pharo (Pharo Park and Palace)

Formerly Napoleon III's local imperial residence, this majestic building and its surrounding gardens offer some of the most spectacular views in the entire city. Be sure to circle around to check out the seascapes and views to the nearby islands. Conferences are now held in the palace, and the park is open daily. ⓐ 58 blvd Charles Livon ⓒ Park open from 09.00–22.00 ⓝ Bus: 81, 83

Saint Victor Abbey

With foundations that date from the 5th century, the Saint Victor Abbey was renovated and rebuilt in the 13th century after barbarian invasions. Visit the extensive underground crypts, where the walnut statue Notre Dame de Confession (commonly referred to as the Black Virgin) is housed. Thousands of pilgrims flock to the Abbey for the yearly Candlemas celebrations (see page 12). ⓣ 04 96 11 22 60 ⓒ 09.00–19.00 ⓝ Metro: 1 to Vieux-Port. Admission charge for crypts

Vallon des Auffes

Take a stroll down to this picturesque fishing port, where brightly coloured cottages are interspersed with a range of excellent restaurants. ⓝ Bus: 83

CULTURE

Musée des Arts Contemporains (Contemporary Art Museum)

Cutting-edge contemporary artworks exhibited in a verdant setting. ⓐ 69 blvd d'Haifa ⓣ 04 91 25 01 07 ⓒ 10.00–17.00 Tues–Sun, Oct–May; 11.00–18.00 Tues–Sun, June–Sept, closed Mon ⓝ Métro: Rond-Point du Prado; bus: 23, 45, 69. Admission charge

---

ⓓ *Peaceful Vallon des Auffes offers a welcome break from the city's bustle*

SOUTH OF THE PORT

Musée Boutique de l'OM (Olympique Marseilles Football Museum)
If football's your passion, check out this little museum dedicated
to the local Marseilles team. ⓐ blvd Michelet, Velodrome Stadium
🕐 10.00–19.00 Mon–Sat, June–Sept; 10.00–13.00, 14.00–18.00
Mon–Sat, Oct–May, closed Sun ⓜ Metro: 2 to Rond-Point du
Prado; bus: 21

RETAIL THERAPY

Alimentation générale Everything for the eclectic foodie,
including lunchboxes, home-made jams and sugar sculptures.
Marseilles' Centre Design is upstairs, and hosts rotating exhibitions.
ⓐ 1 rue de l'Abbaye ☎ 06 64 84 60 48 🕐 10.00–19.00 Tues–Sat,
closed Sun & Mon, Aug ⓜ Metro: 1 to Vieux-Port; bus: 54, 81, 83

🔽 *Try the original orange-blossom biscuits at their birthplace*

MARSEILLES' OLDEST AUTHENTICATED BISCUIT

Biscuit dating is a science that its practitioners find to be fraught with inexactitude, yet there is one item on whose nativity everyone can agree, and that is that the *navette* was born in 1781 in Marseilles in the shop now called the Four des Navettes. Navettes are sweet biscuits flavoured with the extract of orange blossom, and they are formed (roughly) to the shape of rowing boats. Why this should be is the subject for enough debate to make us conclude that nobody really knows. The Four des Navettes is still going strong on the back of them, and does a roaring trade in the basic model and all the variations that have evolved over the years; quite intriguingly, it retains – and uses – the very same oven in which the very first batch of blossom-flavoured beauties was produced.

Four des Navettes ⓐ 136 rue Sainte Anne
ⓦ www.fourdesnavettes.com ⓒ 07.00–20.00 Mon–Sat, 09.00–13.00, 15.00–19.30 Sun, Sept–July; 09.00–13.00, 15.00–19.30 Aug Ⓝ Metro: 1 to Vieux-Port; bus: 54, 81, 83

Tcheka stocks clothes designed by local Marseilles designers, as well as a selection of smaller French brands. Staff are as trendy as they are friendly. ⓐ 5 pl. de la Corderie ⓣ 04 91 33 00 97 ⓒ 13.00–19.00 Mon, 09.00–19.00 Tues–Sat Ⓝ Bus: 55, 81

Temps des Cerises Boutique Hankering after a pair of these made-in-Marseilles jeans? Head to their boutique, located just

---

MARKETS

The markets of this area are special in that they sell products that have often come straight down from the port – and so have the witticisms that pour from the stall-owners.

Produce Market 🚇 pl. Castellane (odd-numbered side)
🕐 08.00–13.00 Mon–Sat , Metro: 1, 2 to Castellane; 2 to Périer

Flower Market 🚇 pl. Castellane (even-numbered side)
🕐 08.00–13.00 Fri , Metro: 1, 2 to Castellane; 2 to Périer

---

off avenue Prado. 🚇 9 rue Haxo 📞 04 91 33 97 78
🌐 www.letempsdescerisesjeans.com 🕐 10.00–19.00
Mon–Sat, closed Sun Ⓜ Metro: 2 to Rond-Point du Prado;
bus: 19, 21, 41S, 73, 74

TAKING A BREAK

Les Akolytes £ ❶ A modern, brightly coloured spot for cool drinks and light snacks, across the street from Les Catalans beach. To try the mix of ethnic dishes, order the €19 menu, which includes four tapas and two desserts. 🚇 41 rue Papety 📞 04 91 59 17 10 🕐 12.00–14.30, 20.00–00.00 Mon & Tues, Thur & Fri; 20.00–00.00 Sat, closed Sat lunch, Wed & Sun Ⓜ Bus: 83

Honoré ££ ❷ Combo restaurant with a boutique in the back, owner Annick designs items like embroidered bags, while the restaurant serves up tapas and light meals. 🚇 121 rue Sainte 📞 04 91 33 08 34 🌐 www.honore-france.com 🕐 Restaurant:

Lunch Tues–Fri, Dinner Thurs–Sat, Boutique: 10.00–19.00
Tues–Sat Ⓝ Metro: 1 to Vieux-Port; bus: 54, 81, 83

AFTER DARK

RESTAURANTS

Chez Fon-Fon ££ ❸ Reputedly a favourite spot of Sean Connery,
Chez Fon-Fon was also featured in the film *The French Connection*
(Fernando Rey stops here). The modern French cuisine includes
reasonably priced *bouillabaisse* in an unbelievably cute location.
ⓐ 14 rue de Vallon des Auffes ❶ 04 91 52 14 38 Ⓦ www.chez-
fonfon.com Ⓛ Lunch Tues–Sat, Dinner Mon–Sat, closed Sun
Ⓝ Bus: 83

Sushi Street Café ££ ❹ Bizarrely set up by an Irishman in
Marseilles, this little spot serves up the best sushi in the city.
ⓐ 24 blvd Notre-Dame ❶ 04 91 54 17 90 Ⓛ Lunch Tues–Fri,
Dinner Tues–Sat, closed Sun Ⓝ Bus: 57

L'Epuisette £££ ❺ Just off the rue de Vallon des Auffes,
L'Epuisette's terrace is almost directly at sea level. One of the
most romantic places around, and outstanding food too, such
as cod infused with scallops' eggs and truffles. Michelin-starred.
ⓐ rue de Vallon des Auffes ❶ 04 91 52 17 82 Ⓦ www.l-epuisette.com
Ⓛ Lunch & dinner Tues–Sat, closed Sun & Mon, Aug Ⓝ Bus: 83

Le Peron £££ ❻ With a beautiful teak terrace, views over the sea
and Ile d'If, you may almost forget that this joint is Michelin-starred
– until you taste the high-end entrées like red tuna in satay and

● *Sea views and sunshine on the terrace of Le Peron*

see the extensive wine list. ⓐ 59 corniche Président John Kennedy ① 04 91 52 15 22 ● 12.00–14.00, 19.30–22.30 Ⓝ Bus: 83

Le Rhul £££ ❼ As one would expect from a founding member of the 'Charte de la Bouillabaisse Marseillaise' (see page 28), the excellent *bouillabaisse* at this seaside locale is apparently favoured by Jacques Chirac and the Rolling Stones. ⓐ 269 corniche Président John Kennedy ① 04 91 52 01 77 Ⓦ www.bouillabaissemarseilles.com ● 12.00–14.00, 19.30–22.00 Ⓝ Bus: 83

BARS & CLUBS

Escale Borély This large waterfront complex houses a wide range of bars, cafés and restaurants. For a trendy take on karaoke, or club nights aimed at a youthful crowd, choose the Café de la Plage. Ⓝ Bus: 83

▶ *Traditional wooden fishing boats line the Cassis harbour*

Cassis & the Calanques

The town of Cassis is a beautiful little fishing village. Although it now earns a living primarily from tourism and its famous AOC (Appellation d'Origine Contrôlée) wine, Cassis' original claim to fame was as an important quarry: the stone quays in Marseilles' Vieux Port come from here (as does the base of the US's Statue of Liberty). The Massif des Calanques, 20 km (12 miles) of rocky coves and cliffs located between Marseilles and Cassis, is really only accessible by boat or on foot. Visiting it can be as adventurous as you wish: there are easy walks in from both ends, or you can scale the heights with radical rock-climbing. Be sure to check for seasonal closures, implemented to prevent forest fires when weather is very dry. Call ☎ 08 11 20 13 13 or check with the tourist office for further information.

GETTING THERE

By rail
Cassis is located 22km (14 1/2 miles) from Marseilles' city centre. Trains between the two cities run four to five times per hour, from 06.00–23.05 (direction Cassis), and from 05.15–22.10 (direction Marseilles). The journey lasts about 30 minutes (🇼 www.ter-sncf.fr). Cassis train station (☎ 36 35) is located 3.5km (2.2 miles) outside the city centre, to which you can walk or take one of the frequent *navettes* (buses, Mon–Sat), or taxis (☎ 04 42 01 78 96). The Calanques cannot be accessed directly by train.

▶ *Rugged cliffs provide shelter in the secluded bay of the Calanque d'En Vau*

Around Marseilles

○	City
○	Large Town
○	Small Town
■	POI
	Motorway
	Main Road
	Minor Road
✈	Airport
	Railway

0   10 km
0   5 miles

🔺 *Pastel colours and fragrant flowers at Cassis' train station*

By road

Buses depart directly for Cassis via the motorway from
place Castellane (Ⓝ Bus: M6, three times per day via motorway
Ⓦ www.lepilote.com). The fastest way to drive to Cassis is on the
A50. Alternatively, take the scenic route by heading out of Marseilles
through the Prado area and boulevard Michelet. Follow the signs
for Cassis along the D559, or stop anywhere along the way to visit
the Calanques of Callelongue, Sormiou and Morgiou. Once you've
arrived at Cassis, park just outside the town centre at Parking
Gorguettes (free) and take the shuttle (€0.50 return) to the main
square. Other (paying) car parks are dotted around the town centre.

By water

To visit the Calanques from Marseilles, contact **Icard Maritime/
Marseilles Cote Mer** (ⓐ 1 quai Marcel Pagnol ❶ 04 91 33 03 29

Ⓦ www.marseille-cote-mer.com). To visit the Calanques from
Cassis, contact **Les Bateliers Cassidains** (Ⓣ 04 42 01 90 83
Ⓦ www.calanques-cassis.com) or head to the yellow hut on
quai Saint-Pierre for daily schedules and tickets. Excursions
depart approximately every 30 minutes, visiting three-to-eight
Calanques by sea. During the summer, you can also choose to
get off at the Calanque d'En Vau (Ⓛ 09.00–11.00). Spend the
morning enjoying the gorgeous beach, then hike your way
back to Cassis (two hours, moderately difficult).

CASSIS

SIGHTS & ATTRACTIONS

Cassis' AOC (Appellation d'Origine Contrôlée) wines are some of
France's most celebrated. The local tourist office (Ⓐ quai des Moulins
Ⓣ 08 92 25 98 92) has information on the 'Vin et Terroir' walk, a stroll
through the vineyards that surround the town. Alternatively,
contact Syndicat des Vignerons de Cassis (Ⓐ Château de Fontcreuse,
13 route de La Ciotat Ⓣ 04 42 01 71 09) to arrange to view one of
the 12 *domains* nearby. Particularly recommended is Domaine
du Paternel's Cassis Blanc, an outstanding wine. Wines from

WHAT 'AOC' MEANS
AOC is nothing more fancy than a quality assurance guarantee.
It signifies that a wine has been produced to a standard
of soil, climate and grape conditions, but – please note –
it makes no promises about the quality of the wine itself.

Clos Sainte-Madeline are popular, as are those from the Domaine des Quatre Vents, particularly the rosés.

CULTURE
Fondation Camargo
Formerly the Hotel Panorama, in 1967 this was purchased by American artist Jerome Hill, and he commenced his residency programme for artists, composers and scholars here. Concerts and lectures, often in English, are held frequently, as is the annual Printemps du Livre. ⓐ av. de l'Amiral Ganteaume ⓣ 04 42 01 11 57 ⓦ www.camargofoundation.org, www.printempsdulivre-cassis.org

Musée Méditerranéen d'Art et Traditions Populaires
For a dose of Provençal artworks and artefacts, head to this little museum, housed in a renovated 17th-century presbytery. ⓐ rue Xavier d'Authier ⓣ 04 42 01 88 66 ⓛ 10.30–12.30, 15.30–18.30 Wed–Sat

⬤ Cassis' brightly coloured townhouses

RETAIL THERAPY

L'Art du Temps Linger over the eclectic choice of painted ceramics, antique restored furniture and Provençal paintings. ⓐ 10 rue Pierre-Eydin ⓣ 04 42 01 88 55 ⓛ 10.00–19.30 Mon–Sat

Maison des Vins If you've fallen in love with the local wines, head to this speciality store to pick up a few bottles. Staying in a self-catering apartment? Pop next door to the Maison des Coquillages for some seafood to have along with your wine. ⓐ route de Marseilles ⓣ 04 42 01 15 61 ⓦ www.maisondesvinscassis.com

Quai des Artistes Here you can pick up local arts and crafts, as well as quirky flowers. ⓐ quai Calendal ⓛ 19.00–24.00 July & Aug

TAKING A BREAK

Sucr'E delices £ Here you'll find gourmet pastries with a touch of imagination. Traditional sweet cakes and biscuits are often flavoured with a blend of fruits, herbs and vegetables. ⓐ 4 rue Alexandre Gervais ⓣ 04 42 03 59 79

Le Chai Cassidain £–££ Pop into this specialist wine bar for a taste of the best local produce. ⓐ 6 rue Séverin Icard ⓣ 04 42 01 99 80 ⓦ www.lechaicassidain.com ⓛ 10.00–22.30 Mon–Sat, closed Sun

AFTER DARK

L'Oustau de la Mar £ Nestled among the restaurants that line the port, L'Oustau de la Mar serves up spectacular seafood and excellent-value three-course menus (€22.50), as well as daily specials like filet of sole doused in a raspberry butter. ⓐ 20 quai des Baux ① 04 42 01 78 22 ② 19.00–22.30, 12.00–14.30 Sat–Wed, closed lunch Thur & Fri, mid-Nov–mid-Dec

Fleurs de Thym ££ Set in the town centre, Fleurs de Thym offers traditional Provençal cuisine made from seasonal local ingredients, like red mullet and sardines, or courgettes and aubergines. ⓐ 5 rue Lamartine ① 04 42 01 23 03 ⓦ www.fleursdethym.com ② 19.00–22.00 Tues–Sun Oct–Mar, closed Mon Oct–Mar & first two weeks of Jan

Nino £££ The Brezzo family have been running this upmarket restaurant on Cassis' port since 1962. The cuisine is modern French, and the décor has a nautical theme. The restaurant also rents chambres d'hôtes, rooms in the picturesque buildings surrounding the port. ⓐ 1 quai Barthelemy ① 04 42 01 74 32 ⓦ www.nino-cassis.com ② Lunch & dinner Tues–Sun, closed Mon & mid-Dec–mid-Feb

ACCOMMODATION

Les Cigales £ Just 1.5km (1 mile) outside of Cassis, this ample campground has 250 sites, and does not accept reservations. ⓐ av. de la Marne ① 04 42 01 07 34 ⓕ 04 42 01 34 18 ⓦ www.campingcassis.com ② closed mid-Nov–mid-Mar

Le Provençal £ The best budget option in Cassis, Le Provençal is located just steps away from the port. For the enthusiastic hiker, breakfast (€6.50) can be delivered to the room from 07.00. ⓐ 7 av. Victor Hugo ① 04 42 01 72 13 ⓕ 04 42 01 39 58 ⓦ www.cassis-le-Provençal.com ⓔ le-Provençal@aliceadsl.fr

Le Jardin d'Emile ££ The atmosphere is relaxed at this little
hotel, just off of the plage de Bestouan; the colourful rooms
and their adjacent patios are immersed in a lush garden.
ⓐ av. de l'Amiral Ganteaume ⓣ 04 42 01 80 55 ⓕ 04 42 01 80 70
ⓦ www.lejardindemile.fr

Les Roches Blanches ££ Formerly a 19th-century fortress, the pretty
rooms of this hotel look out onto the Calanques and the sea.
There is an infinity pool and direct access to the sea. ⓐ route des
Calanques ⓣ 04 42 01 09 30 ⓦ www.roches-blanches-cassis.com

THE CALANQUES

SIGHTS & ATTRACTIONS

The best time to visit the Calanques is during the spring and early
autumn, avoiding the peaks in temperature that can be reached
in this area during the summer months. Note that some Calanques
are closed during summer due to the high risk of forest fires –
check ⓦ www.calanques.fr for further information.

It takes about 11 hours for an experienced walker to cross the
Calanques from Marseilles to Cassis, although there are paths
and routes to suit all ability levels. If you are concerned about
setting out alone, contact the tourist office who will put you in
touch with other hikers heading out together. From Madrague-
de-Montredon, it's a relatively easy hike up to the summit of
the Massif de Marseilleveyre for expansive views of Marseilles's
cityscape. Amble down to the Calanque de Callelongue, where
you can catch the bus back to Marseilles. The Calanque de Sormiou
is a top spot for rock-climbing (ⓦ www.topo-calanques.com).

It used to be a working fishing port, and the cottages that still surround it are now used as holiday homes. The Calanque de Sugiton is accessible and popular with hikers, and is just over an hour's downhill hike from Luminy. The Calanque d'En Vau may win the prize for most beautiful, with its white sandy beach and turquoise waters. Rent a kayak in Cassis (Club Sport Loisirs Nautiques ⓐ pl. Montmorin ⓣ 04 42 01 80 01) and head here for the day.

If the hiking sounds a little too gruelling, both the peaceful Calanque de Port Pin, with its sandy beach, and the Calanque de Port Miou are within an hour's easy amble from Cassis' town centre. Travelling with young children? Try the Sentier du Petit Prince, a gentle walk around the Cap Cable peninsula. Shuttles run from Cassis' Gorguettes car park.

● *Spend an afternoon at one of the area's many beaches*

TAKING A BREAK
Chez La Belge £ A casual place to stop for salads and abundant plates of pasta, about an hour's hike from Callelongue. ⓐ Calanque de Marseillesveyre ⓣ no telephone, reservations in person only ⓛ Lunch June–Aug, Sat & Sun, Sept–May

AFTER DARK
Le Lunch ££ A beautiful seaside locale in the Calanque de Sormiou. Specialities include *bouillabaisse* and freshly caught fish. Reservations are required, as during the summer months automobile access to this Calanque is restricted. ⓣ 04 91 25 05 37 ⓛ closed Nov–mid-Mar ⓘ No credit cards

La Grotte de Callongue ££–£££ All turn-of-the-century French elegance, La Grotte is as famous for its amazing seafood, like the *moules* (mussels), as it is for its long and established history. ⓐ 1 rue Pebrons, Callongue ⓣ 04 91 73 17 79 ⓦ www.lagrotte.fr ⓛ 12.00–14.30 & 20.00–23.00 Mon–Sat

ACCOMMODATION
Auberge de Jeunesse £ The most peaceful spot to bed down for a night in the middle of the Calanques. Sixty dormitory beds are spread over six rooms, and much of the energy comes from solar power. ⓐ La Fontasse ⓣ 04 42 01 02 72 ⓛ closed Jan–mid-Mar

Hotel Mahogany £££ Try and book one of the 19 sea-facing rooms in this hotel built into a tiny calanque. The private terraces come complete with exquisite views. ⓐ plage du Bestouan ⓣ 04 42 01 05 70 ⓕ 04 42 01 34 82 ⓦ www.hotelmahogany.com

Aix-en-Provence

The City of Fountains, Aix-en-Provence was founded in 122 BC, when Sextius Calvinius led the Romans in setting up camp on the site in order to take advantage of the natural hot springs. A mild Provençal town with over 300 sun-dappled days every year, it's no wonder that local boy Cézanne became a world-renowned artist. Visit Aix in June, for the Musique dans la Rue Festival (Music in the Streets Festival, which takes place over France's Fete de la Musique, ● 21 June) or in July for the Festival de Aix-en-Provence (● third week in July).

● *Fontaine de la Rotunde, with its sculpture of Justice, Agriculture and the Arts*

GETTING THERE

By rail

Aix-en-Provence is located approximately 30 km (19 miles) from Marseilles. Trains between the two cities run three to four times per hour, from 05.20–23.15 (direction Aix-en-Provence), and from 05.00–21.30 (direction Marseilles). The train ride is about 50 minutes (ⓦ www.sncf.fr). Aix-en-Provence is also on the TGV line between Paris and Marseilles, and it takes less than three hours to reach France's capital city (ⓦ www.tgv.com), despite the fact that they are over 750km (466 miles) apart! Do note that the TGV station is about 12km (7.5 miles) west of the city centre (as opposed to the centrally located SNCF station). You'll have to hop on one of

the regular shuttle buses to and from the centre of town
(🕒 04.45–22.30, departing every 20 mins).

By road

The bus station, or gare routière, provides frequent access to
Marseilles as well as surrounding towns in Provence (ⓐ av. de
l'Europe ❶ 08 91 02 40 25 🔵 www.lepilote.com 🕒 Buses between
Marseilles and Aix 05.50–23.50, departing every five to ten mins).

Departing from Marseilles, if you're driving head to Aix-en-
Provence on the A51. Exit at Aix centre. During high season, it's
virtually impossible to drive in the city centre or find a place to
park on the streets – your best bet is to leave your car at one of
the large car parks, such as Pasteur ⓐ 16 av. Pasteur

SIGHTS & ATTRACTIONS

Cathédrale Saint-Saveur

Located on the site of a former Roman temple, this eclectic
cathedral was built upon and tweaked over 13 centuries
(5th through to 18th). Note the different architectural styles
of the exterior gates, and the three radically different naves
(Romanesque, Gothic and baroque).

Thermes Sextius

Be like former bathers Pablo Picasso and Winston Churchill and
pop into the Sextius Thermal Baths for a day of treatments and
relaxation. Be sure to check out the remains of the ancient

🔘 *The city's famous Cathédrale Saint-Saveur*

thermal pool at the entrance. Daily treatments start at €84.
a 55 cours Sextius **t** 04 42 23 81 82 **f** 04 42 95 11 33
w www.thermes-sextius.com

CULTURE

Musée Granet

Located in the 16th-century Priory of the Knights of Malta, the renovated Musée Granet holds an exceptional collection of paintings by French artists during the 17th–19th centuries. There is also a 'Cézanne Room' dedicated to contemplation of nine of the artist's oils, and a small collection of modern art. **a** pl. Saint Jean de Malte **t** 04 42 52 88 32 **w** www.muséegranet-aixenprovence.fr

PAUL CÉZANNE

Around these parts, there's no danger of forgetting that Cézanne is Aix's most famous son. Visit the Aix-en-Provence tourist office (**a** 2 pl. du General de Gaulle **t** 04 42 16 11 61 **f** 04 42 16 11 62 **w** www.aixenprovencetourism.com **c** 08.30–19.00 Mon–Sat, 10.00–13.00, 14.00–18.00 Sun) to arrange tickets and visits to Jas de Bouffan Manor, the family house purchased by Cézanne's father when the artist was 20, and Cézanne's studio at Les Lauves, which was built to the artist's specifications in 1902. Décor has been arranged as it was upon Cézanne's death. Alternatively, book a day-long Cézanne Tour, again through the tourist office (**t** 04 42 16 11 61 **w** www.atelier-cezanne.com).

⬥ *Mount Sainte-Victoire, just outside Aix, was one of Cézanne's favourite subjects*

🕐 11.00–19.00 Tues–Sun, June–Sept; 12.00–18.00 Tues–Sun, Oct–May, closed Mon 🚌 Bus: 4. Admission charge

Musée de Tapisseries (Museum of Tapestries)
Visit an outstanding collection of 17th- and 18th-century tapestries, including the unique 'History of Don Quichotte' tapestry, which dates from 1735. 🅐 Palais de l'Archêveché, 28 pl. des Martyrs de la Résistance 📞 04 42 23 09 91 🕐 10.00–18.00 Wed–Sun mid-Apr–mid-Oct; 13.30–17.00 Wed–Sun, mid-Oct–mid-Apr, closed Tues, Jan

RETAIL THERAPY

Genis Be sure to try *calissons*, a sweet speciality of Aix that consists of ground almonds, fruit syrup and a frosted wafer biscuit. Step

AIX MARKETS

Don't miss the daily Produce Market (🕑 08.00–12.30), under the plane trees in place Richelme. Keep an eye out for local producers, who often organise visiting days to their farms (advertised somewhere on their market stall) during key harvest times. Pick up second-hand goods and clothes, as well as fruits and vegetables, at the large market in place des Prêcheurs and place de la Madeleine, with antiques concentrated in place de Verdun (🕑 08.00–12.30 Tues, Thur & Sat). Wander through the Flower Market to smell the Provençal countryside (🅐 pl. de l'Hôtel de Ville 🕑 08.00–12.30 Tues, Thur & Sat; 🅐 pl. des Prêcheurs 🕑 08.00–12.30 Wed, Fri, Sun & Mon). During the summer, hit the arts and crafts market in the evening along cours Mirabeau.

⬤ *Early morning at the flower market in Aix*

into old-style Genis to pick up a home-made sack-full. ⓐ 1 rue
Gaston de Saporta ⓣⓕ 04 42 23 30 64 ⓛ 09.00–19.00

TAKING A BREAK

Unic Bar £ Go for the €5 breakfast and enjoy the morning
action at the local producers' market. ⓐ 40 rue Vauvenargues,
on pl. Richelme ⓣ 04 42 96 38 28 ⓛ 07.00–24.00

Le Café des Deux Garçons ££ Founded in 1792, this café was
frequented daily by Cézanne and his good friend Emile Zola,
(also from Aix). Stop in for an aperitif on the ample terrace.
ⓐ 53 cours Mirabeau ⓣ 04 42 26 00 51 ⓛ 07.00–02.00

AFTER DARK

RESTAURANTS
Geisha Sushi Experience £–££ Linger over outstanding sushi,
best enjoyed by candle light on the terrace, next door to Cézanne's
father's former hat shop. ⓐ 53 cours Mirabeau ⓣ 04 42 20 30 00
ⓛ 10.00–24.00

Le Zinc d'Hugo £–££ Tucked away from the bustling crowds,
this tiny restaurant creates simmering bistro specialities in
a cosy atmosphere. This is the perfect spot on a chilly night.
ⓐ 22 rue Lieutaud ⓣ 04 42 27 69 69 ⓛ Lunch & dinner Tues–Sat

Chez Antoine Cote Cour ££ Dine in the plant-filled interior
courtyard of Chez Antoine, located just off the cours Mirabeau.

> **PINK PASSION**
>
> Are you crazy about salmon? Head to the **Le Saumon Passion ££** 🅐 55 rue Espariat 🕿 04 42 26 73 73 🕘 09.00–19.00 Tues–Sat. At this combination deli and tiny restaurant, you can taste pretty much any variety of salmon (Danish, Irish, Norwegian, Baltic...) in any form (wild, marinated, smoked, tarama...) as well as many other types of cured fish and caviar.

The menu blends Italian and Provençal dishes, focusing on seafood and seasonal specialities. 🅐 19 cours Mirabeau 🕿 04 42 93 12 51 🕘 Lunch Tues–Sat, Dinner Mon–Sat

Le Clos des Violettes £££ Michelin-starred Chef Jean-Marc Banzo whips up exquisite haute cuisine in what is arguably the best restaurant in Aix. Reservations required. 🅐 10 av. de la Violette 🕿 04 42 23 30 71 🆆 www.closdelaviolette.com 🕘 Lunch & dinner Tues–Sat

ACCOMMODATION

Aix offers a wealth of options for accommodation in or near the city. Check the list below, or alternatively, contact the central Accommodation Booking Office at Aix's tourist office for assistance with direct reservations. 🅐 Office de Tourisme, 2 pl. du General-de-Gaulle, first floor 🕿 04 42 16 11 84 🆒 04 42 16 11 79 🅔 resaix@aixenprovencetourism.com

Hotel Cardinal £ Situated on a sleepy residential road, just across from the Musée Granet, the Hotel Cardinal's flowery French décor is both elegant and charming. Book a double room, or one of their six suites, each with kitchenette. ⓐ 24 rue Cardinale ⓣ 04 42 38 32 30 ⓕ 04 42 26 39 05 ⓦ www.hotel-cardinal-aix.com

Hotel de France £ Just around the corner from Aix's central Rotonde, this little hotel is a bargain spot to bed down for the night. Walls are a cheery yellow, and temporary art exhibitions are held on the first floor. Some rooms may be a little on the small side. Cosy, then. ⓐ 63 rue Espariat ⓣ 04 42 27 90 15 ⓕ 04 42 26 11 47 ⓦ www.hoteldefrance-aix.com

○ Linger like the locals at one of Aix's many pavement cafés

Hotel des Augustins ££ This was formerly a 7th-century convent, and Martin Luther chose to stay here for weeks after his excommunication by the Catholic Church. Perfectly located just off the cours Mirabeau, each of the 29 rooms retains many period features, such as original stonework and antique tiles. ⓐ 3 rue de la Masse ⓣ 04 42 27 28 59 ⓕ 04 42 26 74 87 ⓦ www.hotel-augustins.com ⓔ hotel.augustins@wanadoo.fr

Aquabella Hotel ££–£££ With direct access to the ancient Thermes Sextius Roman thermal baths (as well as the sauna, hammam and heated pool), book a self-indulgent weekend at this modern hotel. ⓐ 2 rue des Étuves ⓣ 04 42 99 15 00 ⓕ 04 42 99 15 07 ⓦ www.aquabella.fr

Le Pigonnet £££ At the turn of the century, Cézanne painted Mount Sainte-Victoire from the picturesque garden of this Provençal house. Small and utterly luxurious, with clientele to match. ⓐ 5 av. du Pigonnet ⓣ 04 42 59 02 90 ⓕ 04 42 59 47 77 ⓦ www.hotelpigonnet.com ⓔ reservation@hotelpigonnet.com

◗ Marseilles is France's largest and most important port

Directory

GETTING THERE

By air

Marseilles Provence Airport is the fourth-busiest in France. Twenty-five airlines offer direct flights to almost 100 cities worldwide, including **British Airways** (📞 08 25 82 54 00 🌐 www.britishairways.com (to London Gatwick)), **Airlingus** (📞 08 21 23 02 67 🌐 www.aerlingus.com (to Dublin)) and **Air France** (to Paris, Lisbon, Milan, Rome and Tunis). It is also possible to fly directly to Montréal with **Air Transat** (📞 08 25 12 02 48 🌐 www.airtransat.ca). Terminal 2 (MP2) was opened at the end of 2006 to service low-cost carriers, including **Ryanair** (📞 08 92 23 23 75 🌐 www.ryanair.com (to London Stansted, Bournemouth, Glasgow, Dublin and Madrid, as well as Marrakech and Fès from Oct 2007)), **BmiBaby** (📞 08 90 71 00 81 🌐 www.bmibaby.com (to Birmingham)) and **easyJet** (📞 08 26 10 26 11 🌐 www.easyjet.com (to London Gatwick and Bristol)).

Many people are aware that air travel emits CO_2, which contributes to climate change. You may be interested in the possibility of lessening the environmental impact of your flight through Climate Care, which offsets your CO_2 by funding environmental projects around the world. Visit 🌐 www.climatecare.org

By rail

Since the end of 2007, Eurostar trains have departed for Paris Gare du Nord from London's renovated St Pancras station. Hop on one of the 17 daily high-speed TGV trains direct from Paris, the fastest reaching Marseilles' Gare Saint-Charles in just under three hours. If you're arriving from other cities in Europe, check Ⓦ www.raileurope.com for general rail information, or Ⓦ www.voyages-sncf.fr for details regarding train travel in France. The monthly *Thomas Cook European Rail Timetable* has up-to-date schedules for European international and national train services. For **Eurostar** reservations (UK) ☎ 08705 186 186 Ⓦ www.eurostar.com

Thomas Cook European Rail Timetable ☎ (UK) 01733 416477, (USA) 1 800 322 3834 Ⓦ www.thomascookpublishing.com

🔺 *Upon exiting the Gare Saint-Charles, the city spills below your feet*

By road

Driving from the UK, it will take approximately two days to cover the 1,200km (720 miles) from London to Marseilles. Head to Paris, and follow the A6, then the A7 to Marseilles. For driving into Marseilles' city centre, see page 51.

Marseilles' main bus station, the gare routière, is well connected to most major European cities. For specific information regarding schedules and prices, check:

National Express ☎ 08 70 58 08 080
🅦 www.nationalexpress.com (UK)
Eurolines ☎ 04 91 50 57 55 🅦 www.infociao.com (Marseilles)

By water

Marseilles' commercial port offers frequent ferries to five destinations in Corsica, including Bastia, Calvi and Ajaccio, as well as Porto Torres in Sardinia and Tunis in Tunisia. For information and timetables, check SNCM Ferries (🅦 www.sncm.fr). Prices vary according to season and special offers. Journey times range from approximately 11 to 27 hours.

ENTRY FORMALITIES

Citizens of the European Union must show a passport or national identity card upon entrance into France. Visas are not required for tourists from the UK, Ireland, USA, Canada Australia or New Zealand who plan to remain in France for less than 90 days. For further details, or if you have doubts as to whether you may require a visa, contact the French embassy or consulate closest to your home, or check
🅦 www.diplomatie.gouv.fr

Residents of the UK, Ireland and other EU countries may bring tobacco and alcohol for personal use into France. Residents of non-EU countries, and EU residents arriving from a non-EU country, may bring in up to 400 cigarettes and 50 cigars or 50g (2 oz) tobacco; two litres (three bottles) of wine and one litre (approx. two pints) of spirits or liqueurs. The full regulations, as well as definitions of goods for personal use, are detailed on ⓦ www.douane.gouv.fr

MONEY

The euro (€) is the official currency in France. €1 = 100 cents. Notes are €5, €10, €20, €50, €100, €200 and €500, while coins are broken down into denominations of €1 and €2, and 1, 2, 5, 10, 20 and 50 cents.

ATM machines can be found at the airport, railway stations, outside most banks and pretty much on every second or third corner in the city centre. Most accept British and international debit and credit cards. To be on the safe side, ensure that your card has a chip and a pin (often required). ATM machines are the quickest and most convenient way to obtain euros. Instructions on use are usually available in English and other major European languages.

Both VISA and MasterCard are widely accepted; American Express is sometimes accepted, although not always. Traveller's cheques have become relatively difficult to cash in recent years, even at banks – seek out a bureau de change (there is one at the airport, or see below). Foreign currencies can be cashed at most banks and bureaux de change – you may have to produce your passport or other ID. American Express' bureau de change is located in the centre of the city ⓐ 39 La Canebière ⓣ 04 91 13 71 21 ⓛ 08.00–18.00 Mon–Fri, 08.30–12.00, 14.00–16.30 Sat

HEALTH, SAFETY & CRIME

Marseilles is a relatively safe city. There really aren't any food and drink precautions that need to be taken, other than ensuring you don't consume excessively! Tap water is fine for drinking, although many people prefer bottled mineral water. Health care ranges from adequate to very good, and emergency services are provided to anyone who needs them. If you are a European citizen or permanent resident, be sure to pack your European Health Insurance Card (EHIC) any time you travel – emergency health care in France will be covered, due to reciprocal European agreements. You may be required to pay for care directly, and you will be reimbursed upon arrival in your home country.

The biggest crime risks for tourists tend to be pickpockets and bag-snatchers – keep your valuables out of sight, and purses should

◓ Local police are friendly and helpful

be zipped up and kept snugly against your body. Dimly lit back streets and the area around the train stations should be avoided at night, particularly if you are alone. Single female visitors should expect that they will be invited for coffee by many a stranger throughout the day. Don't be embarrassed to ignore the invitation and simply walk away. Police in uniform patrol all areas of the city, but tend to keep a low profile.

See Emergencies (page 138) for additional information.

Central Police Station ⓐ 2 rue Antoine Becker ⓣ 04 91 39 80 00. ⓛ 24 hrs ⓝ Bus: 49a, 49b

OPENING HOURS

Shops are normally open 10.00–19.00 Mon–Sat, often with a one- to two-hour break for lunch (around 13.00–15.00, although most shops on the city's main shopping streets do not take this break, and may stay open later). Banks are open approximately 08.30–12.00, 13.30–17.00 Mon–Fri. Restaurants usually serve lunch 12.30–14.30 and dinner 19.30–22.30, although in the city centre restaurants may also be open later or serve all day. Most museums are closed on Monday.

TOILETS

There are public toilets in most public spaces, ranging from coin-operated cabins to crowded cubicles in train stations or shopping centres. You will normally have to pay €0.30–0.50 per person to use these toilets. Stop for a coffee and you can use any café's toilet free of charge, although facilities may be basic. In an emergency, most hotels will allow you to use their toilet (if you look desperate enough!).

CHILDREN

Marseilles' centre is chaotic, and it tends to be difficult to spend prolonged periods of time with young children in the city, unless days are peppered with child-friendly breaks and excursions. That said, there's plenty to do with enthusiastic kids and a little imagination. Try heading to one of the city's many parks, like the Borély Park (🕐 06.00–21.00), with its botanical gardens, the Jardin du Pharo or the Parc Longchamp. In the summer season, visit Les Catalans Beach and the Roucas Blanc beach at the Parc du Prado – both have sandy beaches suitable for children. Museums such as Musée Cantini (see page 83) often stage afternoon courses for children interested in art. If your family's French is up to scratch, visit **La Baleine qui dit 'Vagues'** (ⓐ 50 cours Julien ⓣ 04 91 48 95 60 ⓕ 04 91 47 94 22 ⓦ labaleinequiditvagues.org ⓝ Metro: 1 to Canebière-Réformés) for children's theatre. Alternately, check ⓦ www.ideesdenfants.com, which lists up to date activities and ideas for children of all ages.

Overall, Marseilles is welcoming to children in restaurants, and all baby products, such as food and nappies, can be purchased in small and large supermarkets.

COMMUNICATIONS

Internet

Most hotels are now equipped with high-speed internet connections, and often have Wi-Fi, or wireless connections, as well. Check post offices and libraries for additional internet points, or visit one of the city's many internet cafés, such as:
Info Café ⓐ 1 quai Rive Neuve ⓣ 04 91 33 74 98 ⓞ 09.00–22.00 Mon–Sat, 14.30–19.30 Sun ⓝ Metro: 1 to Vieux-Port

TELEPHONING ABROAD
Dial 00, followed by your country code (UK 44, Republic of Ireland 353, USA and Canada 1, Australia 61, New Zealand 64, South Africa 27) and then the area code (leaving out the first '0' if there is one) and the number.

Phone

To make calls on public telephones, buy phone cards (télécartes) at tabacs (newsagent/tobacconist shops sporting a red diamond sign outside). Note that 0 800 numbers are toll-free within France, while numbers that begin simply 08 are often charged at a higher rate than normal. You can receive telephone calls at public phones with a blue bell symbol on them. If you travel to France often, it may be worth purchasing a French SIM card for your mobile (visit any SFr or Orange mobile phone store for options). All European mobile phones should work in France. If you're travelling from overseas, it's worth checking with your local provider before your travels to ensure coverage.

The area code for Marseilles is 04, followed by an eight-digit number. When dialling from anywhere within France, dial all 10 digits. To call Marseilles from abroad, dial 00 (from Europe), 011 (from the US) or 0011 (from Australia), followed by 33 4 and the eight-digit number.

Post

Postal services in France are reliable. Buy stamps at post offices or tobacconist shops (again, look for the red diamond outside).

Sometimes it's also possible to buy stamps at the shops that sell postcards, although you may be required to have actually purchased your postcards in that particular shop. Marseilles' main post office is located at ⓐ 1 pl. Hôtel des Postes (Ⓜ Metro: 1 to Colbert) behind the Centre Bourse shopping centre, but additional post offices are found throughout the city. You can post letters and postcards in the yellow post boxes affixed to building walls at regular intervals around Marseilles.

ELECTRICITY

France runs on 220v with two-pin plugs. British appliances will need a simple adaptor, easily obtained at any electrical or hardware store in Marseilles or at the airport during your travels. US and other equipment designed for 110v will need a *transformateur* (transformer).

TRAVELLERS WITH DISABILITIES

Most public spaces and larger hotels are well equipped with access and facilities adapted for visitors with mobility problems. Pavements in the city centre tend to be wide and road crossings are wheelchair-accessible. However all facilities are not standardised, and access can be difficult in narrow back streets and smaller towns outside of Marseilles. Useful organisations for advice and information include:

RADAR The principal UK forum for people with disabilities. ⓐ 12 City Forum, 250 City Road, London EC1V 8AF ❶ (020) 7250 0212 Ⓦ www.radar.org.uk

SATH (Society for Accessible Travel & Hospitality) advises US-based travellers with disabilities. ⓐ 347 Fifth Ave, Suite 610, New York, NY 10016 ❶ (212) 447 7284 ❶ (212) 725 8253 Ⓦ www.sath.org

TOURIST INFORMATION

Marseilles' main tourist office is located just behind the Vieux Port, and is well stocked with information, maps and local literature. They also organise guided tours of the city.

Office du Tourisme et des Congrès ⓐ 4 La Canebière
ⓣ 04 91 13 89 00 ⓕ 04 91 13 89 20 ⓦ www.marseille-tourisme.com
ⓔ info@marseille-tourisme.com ⓛ 09.00–20.00 Mon–Sat,
10.00–18.00 Sun, July–Sept; 09.00–19.00 Mon–Sat,
10.00–17.00 Sun, Oct–June

There are also three tourist office kiosks in the city:
ⓐ Gare Saint-Charles ⓣ 04 91 50 59 18
ⓐ 20 rue des Pistoles ⓣ 04 91 90 53 39
ⓐ Villa Mistral, 122 plage de l'Estaque ⓣ 04 91 13 89 00

The following websites provide additional useful information about Marseilles and the surrounding areas:
ⓦ www.marseilles-france.com
ⓦ www.provencetourism.com
ⓦ www.visitprovence.com

BACKGROUND READING

Marius, Fanny, and César by Marcel Pagnol. This trilogy will grab you and immerse you lovingly in Marseilles' culture.
The Count of Monte Cristo by Alexandre Dumas. This, possibly the best-ever story of revenge, is set on the Ile d'If, off the city's coast.
Cyrano de Bergerac by Edmond Rostand. This classic tale shows that, ultimately, the pen is mightier than the nose.

Emergencies

The following are emergency free-call numbers:

Ambulance (SAMU) 🛈 15

Fire Brigade (Pompiers) 🛈 18

Police (Gendarmerie) 🛈 17

Any emergency if calling from a mobile phone 🛈 112

MEDICAL SERVICES

If you have a medical situation that needs attention urgently, either call one of the emergency numbers below, or visit a hospital emergency room. Don't forget to keep proof of payment, in order to be reimbursed by your insurance when you arrive home.

Emergency doctor 🛈 04 91 52 91 52

Emergency dentist 🛈 04 91 85 39 39

Poison Treatment Centre 🛈 04 91 75 25 25

POLICE

Should you lose your wallet, or if any of your valuables are stolen, go directly to the police station in order to make an official declaration. You may need this document in order to make insurance claims, or to request duplicates of documents.

Central Police Station 🅐 2 rue Antoine Becker 🛈 04 91 39 80 00
🕐 Open 24 hrs a day Ⓝ Bus: 49a, 49b

Noailles Police Station 🅐 66 La Canebière 🛈 04 88 77 58 00
Ⓝ Metro: 2 to Noailles

Lost property

Hoping someone has turned in your missing item? Head to the
Lost and Found Ⓐ 41 blvd de Briancon ☎ 04 91 14 68 97 🕒 Mon–Fri

EMBASSIES & CONSULATES

Australia Ⓐ 4 rue Jean Rey, Paris ☎ 01 40 59 33 00
🌐 www.france.embassy.gov.au
Canada Ⓐ 35 av. Montaigne, Paris ☎ 01 44 43 29 00
🌐 www.international.gc.ca/canada
New Zealand Ⓐ 7 rue Léonard da Vinci, Paris ☎ 01 45 01 43 43
🌐 www.nzembassy.com
Republic of Ireland Ⓐ 4 rue Rude, Paris ☎ 01 44 17 67 00
🌐 ireland.visahq.com/embassy/france
South Africa Ⓐ 59 quai d'Orsay, Paris ☎ 01 53 59 23 23
🌐 www.afriquesud.net
UK Consulate General Ⓐ 24 av. du Prado, Marseilles ☎ 04 91 15 72 10
🌐 www.britishembassy.gov.uk
USA Consulate Ⓐ 12 blvd Paul Peytral, Marseilles ☎ 04 91 54 92 00
🌐 www.amb-usa.fr

EMERGENCY PHRASES

Help!   Au secours!   *Or secoors!*

Call the police/fire service/ambulance!
Appelez la police/les pompiers/un ambulance!
Appeley la police/leh pompee-eh/un ambulance!